HUSBANDS & FATHERS

REDISCOVER THE CREATOR'S PURPOSE *for* MEN

Derek Prince

Foreword by Dr. Edwin Louis Cole

Chosen Books

A Division of Baker Book House Co
Grand Rapids, Michigan 49516

Published by Chosen Books
A division of Baker Book House Company
P.O. Box 6287, Grand Rapids, MI 49516-6287

Fourth printing, September 2001

Printed in the United States of America

Library of Congress Cataloging-in-Publication Data

Prince, Derek.
    Husbands and fathers : rediscover the Creator's purpose for
men / Derek Prince.
        p.   cm.
    ISBN 0-8007-9274-2 (pbk.)
      1. Christian men—Religious life. 2. Husbands—Religious life.
3. Fathers—Religious life. I. Title.
    BV4528.2.P75 2000
    248.8'421—dc21   99–38439

All royalties for this book have been assigned to Derek Prince Ministries.

For current information about all releases from Baker Book House, visit our web site:
                    http://www.bakerbooks.com

Contents

Foreword

People hear what you say but learn from what you are. That is true when you read or listen to Derek Prince. He imparts his life into his work, and we are all the better for it.

Derek has written a book that is to be read not just by the father, but by the father to his whole family. God bless him for making God's truth available to us all.

Dr. Edwin Louis Cole
Founder and President
Christian Men's Network

PART 1

Personal

1

How I Became a Father

Looking back over my childhood and early life, I am surprised to find myself writing this book. Very little in that period would seem to qualify me for such a task!

I was born into a British military family, with no brothers or sisters. Every male relative I have ever known has been an officer in the British Army. At the age of nine, suitably attired in a tweed suit and bowler hat, I was sent off to a prep school. From there I went on to Eton, and from there to King's College, Cambridge. For fifteen years I attended various boarding schools, never spending more than three months of any year at home. After five years at Cambridge I wrote a thesis, "The Evolution of Plato's Method of Definition," and was elected to a Fellowship at King's College.

During all the years of my education, I never had a female teacher. At Cambridge I had a few girlfriends, but the inner workings of the female personality remained a mystery to me—a mystery I was not particularly interested in trying to solve!

What promised to be an uneventful career in the rarefied atmosphere of a major university was rudely interrupted by World War II. When my call up to the forces came, I chose a noncombatant role in the British Royal Army Medical Corps. In the Army I decided to continue my academic career by studying the Bible, which I approached purely as a work of philosophy. I found it hard to understand in many places, but determined to read it all the way through from Genesis to Revelation. Then I would be in a position to pronounce an authoritative judgment on it.

After about nine months, somewhere in the book of Job, I had an unexpected encounter with the Bible's author, who revealed Himself to me through the Person of Jesus Christ. That encounter changed the course of my life radically and permanently. After all, I recalled that Plato himself had acknowledged, "We have no word from God," whereas the Bible plainly claimed that it was just that—"the Word of God." The more I studied it and applied it in my daily life, the more convinced I became that its claim was true. It really was God's revelation of Himself to man.

Shortly afterward the Army sent me to the Middle East. After three years in the deserts of Egypt, Libya and the Sudan, I was posted to Jerusalem. There I met and married a Danish schoolteacher, Lydia Christensen. Lydia had been enjoying a successful career as a teacher in the state school system of Denmark when God directed her to leave everything behind and go to Jerusalem. There she opened a faith home for children without parents.

When Lydia and I were married, she brought with her eight girls without parents to whom she had become an adoptive mother, and for whom, from that time onward, I accepted the responsibility of fatherhood. Of these girls, six were Jewish, one was Arab and one was English. They ranged in age from eighteen to three.

How I Became a Father

From my background as a boy without brothers or sisters, I suddenly found myself the only male responsible for ten females—Lydia, her eight girls and one Arab maid, Jameela. In our new relationship we all had many adjustments to make. There were times when I felt that the responsibility I had taken on was too great. Undoubtedly Lydia, too, must have wondered sometimes whether she had made the right decision in marrying me. But somehow the love and grace of God always carried us through.

In addition to these adjustments in our relationships, Lydia and I faced many external pressures. In the first two years of our marriage, we were caught up in the fighting that brought the State of Israel into being. Twice during that time, in order to save our lives, we had to flee from our home in the middle of the night. We were never able to return to either home.

At one point the four older girls were separated from us, but God kept His hand on us and brought us all together again in England as a united family.

Later, after all but the two youngest girls had grown up, Lydia and I spent five years in Kenya, where I served as principal of a training college for African teachers. During this period we adopted a ninth child, an African baby girl. Her mother had died giving birth and the baby had been found abandoned on the mud floor of an African hut.

Three years after Lydia was called home to the Lord, I married my second wife, Ruth. We were married for twenty years, until Ruth in her turn was called home. Ruth added to our union three more adopted children, all of whom are Jewish. So now I stand in the relationship of father to exactly a dozen persons!

Ruth's warm, outgoing personality quickly endeared her to the other members of my family. She also contributed special administrative and editorial skills, which wonderfully complemented my own ministry as a Bible teacher. In the twenty years we were married, my ministry expanded in ways I would never have dreamed of. Through the combined channels of printed books, audiotapes, videotapes, radio and television broadcasting, my Bible teaching has reached into all the continents, even including Antarctica. My office staff tell me that we are now sending our material to every nation to which the U.S. Postal Service delivers, and that portions of my material have been translated into sixty foreign languages.

Our family continues to grow at a rate that is difficult to keep up with. Including additions by marriages and births, the combined family presently numbers about 150 persons! We now have family members residing in many different countries: Israel, Britain, Canada, the United States and Australia. With so large a family so widely scattered, it is not possible for us all to keep in as close contact with each other as we would wish. Nevertheless we still do have the feeling that *we are one family*.

I have not been a perfect husband or father, by any means. But my family life on the whole has been happy and successful, for which I give God all the glory. Through it I have learned many lessons, which I believe God wants me to share in this book.

I look back to a period in my ministry, however, when I came perilously close to missing God's plan for my marriage and my family. At the time I was traveling continually from meeting to meeting and conference to conference, preaching to large crowds and finding a good response from the people. One evening at a conference I heard another speaker make this remark: "The expert is the man away from home with a briefcase."

Those words struck my heart like an arrow.

That really describes me, I thought to myself. *I'm a man away from home with a briefcase. Everybody regards me as an expert. But in actual fact, what's happening in my home?*

God challenged me in an altogether new way that I had to succeed, first and foremost, as a husband and father before I could succeed in any other capacity.

So I began to analyze my own motives. Why did I spend so much time traveling? Why was I so stimulated by appearing in all those meetings? Gradually I recognized in my motives a strong element of personal ambition. I enjoyed standing on the platform in front of a large audience. I basked in my reputation as an "anointed" speaker.

Looking back over my years in public ministry, I recognized that I was more concerned at times about my reputation as a preacher than about some of Lydia's personal and emotional needs. Sometimes I was more concerned about my success as a minister than about the well-being of my family.

By the mercy of God no serious crisis erupted in our home. In fact, my family at times were more loyal to me than I deserved. Today I thank God continually for all of them! I have gradually come to see, however, that personal ambition at the expense of home life is a serious problem in the lives of many men. Some would be considered successful and would consider themselves successful. Yet an inner core of self-centeredness keeps them from the warm, open interchange with their families that is the essence of successful relationships within a home.

There may be no open crisis or thought of the marriage breaking up. Yet the home provides none of the security and fulfillment that the family members need. In many cases the father has so many commitments outside his home that he is not even aware that he is failing his family.

I have come to the conclusion that many men in our contemporary culture need to face this issue. They may be successful in various fields—as bank presidents or doctors or lawyers or computer technicians or on the golf course.

They may even be successful in Christian ministry. Yet they are failures in their own homes.

I want to suggest to you that to succeed in other capacities and to fail as a husband or father is, in God's sight, to fail. No other success can make up for that failure.

I have said many times that the number-one problem in society today is delinquent males—men who have failed in their two primary responsibilities: as husbands and as fathers.

You can read various books about the family, but you cannot build a truly successful family until you understand these two basic roles: husband and father. They are the essential foundation on which a truly happy and harmonious home can be built.

It is my purpose in this book to show you in simple, practical terms what it takes to be a successful husband and a successful father. From there you can go on to achieve true success in any one of many different areas. But above all you will be a blessing to those closest to you—your wife and your children.

PART 2

Husbands

2

Marriage Is a Covenant

To lay a foundation for what I have to say about husbands, I will begin by speaking about marriage, because it is only through marriage that a man becomes a husband.

The three most important permanent relationships available to human beings are:

1. The relationship of the believer to God
2. The relationship between spouses
3. The relationship of believers to one another

Children who are the fruit of a covenant between a man and his wife are thereby included within the scope of the covenant established before God by their parents.

The basis of each of these relationships is a covenant, which is the most solemn, binding form of commitment that the Bible describes. No lasting relationship can be built according to biblical principles without a covenant.

Two main passages in the Bible demonstrate that marriage is a covenant. First we see that wisdom will

> deliver you from the immoral woman, from the seductress who flatters with her words, who forsakes the companion of her youth, and forgets the *covenant* of her God.
>
> Proverbs 2:16–17, emphasis added

17

This passage is saying that the woman who is unfaithful to her husband forgets or breaks the covenant she made with that man before God. Marriage is a covenant, then, between a man and woman, made before God.

Again, in the book of Malachi, God refers to the covenant quality of marriage. The Israelites had been complaining, "We're praying all the time. We're always in the Temple. So why, God, don't You answer our prayers?" God replies:

> You say, "For what reason?" Because the LORD has been witness between you and the wife of your youth, with whom you have dealt treacherously; yet she is your companion and your wife by *covenant*.
>
> Malachi 2:14, emphasis added

So God is speaking in this passage to husbands who deal "treacherously" with their wives—in contemporary language, who cheat on their wives. God is saying, "It doesn't matter how frequently you pray or how much time you spend in church. If you are not faithful to your covenant commitment to your wife, I will not listen to your prayers." Such men, God declares, are covenant-breakers.

For both men and women, therefore, unfaithfulness to the marriage commitment is breaking a covenant. That is why adultery is much more serious a sin than fornication. Fornication—immorality between two unmarried persons— is sin, but it does not break a covenant. Adultery, however, is immorality that does break a covenant. That is what makes it so much more serious a sin.

The Mystery of Covenant

Covenant is one of God's secrets. No one can understand covenant in the biblical sense except by revelation. Only

God can enable us to understand through Scripture what covenant is. The psalmist says:

> The secret of the Lord is with those who fear Him, and *He will show them His covenant.*
>
> Psalm 25:14, emphasis added

So covenant is one of God's secrets that He reveals only to those who fear Him. God-fearing people are the ones who can apprehend and enter into covenant.

In Ephesians 5:22–31 Paul says that the marriage relationship between a man and his wife is a type, or picture, of the relationship between Christ and His Church. Then he adds, "This is a great mystery" (verse 32)—or "This mystery is great." We need to understand the special meaning of the word *mystery* as Paul uses it in this passage.

The people of that time had what they called "mystery religions." These religions offered special secrets only to those who passed through a closely guarded process of initiation. Unless you had been initiated, you could not learn their secrets. When Paul describes marriage as a "mystery," therefore, he implies that we can understand its true nature only if we have passed through the appropriate process of initiation. This process takes place when, by the marriage ceremony, a man and woman enter into covenant with God and with each other. Only when they are willing to make this covenant commitment can they begin to discover the true nature of marriage. Couples not willing to fulfill this condition can experience the legal and physical aspects of marriage, but its true nature remains closed to them. It is still a mystery—a secret.

We need to remember, too, that marriage is not merely a social contract on the human level. Originally and primarily marriage is a biblical concept. To enter into the mystery of marriage, we must first understand what the Bible means by a "covenant." It will be helpful, therefore, to study briefly the principles that apply to all the covenants of the Bible.

The Principles of Covenant

We will look at God's revelation of covenant in successive passages of Scripture from the Psalms, Hebrews and Genesis.

The following passage from the Psalms reveals the kind of people with whom God makes a covenant:

> He [the LORD] shall call to the heavens from above, and to the earth, that He may judge His people: "Gather My saints [My holy ones] together to Me, those who have made a *covenant* with Me by sacrifice."
>
> Psalm 50:4–5, emphasis added

Who are God's saints, His holy ones? The Bible says they are those who have made a covenant with Him on the basis of a sacrifice. Every covenant must be based on a sacrifice.

In Hebrew you would actually say that you *cut*, rather than *make*, a covenant. The word imagery suggests a sharp knife and the shedding of blood. It is just one more reminder that a covenant requires a sacrifice, and a sacrifice requires shed blood—a life laid down.

In Hebrews 9:16–17 the writer says that a testament, or will, comes into force only when a person dies. But the Greek word here translated "testament" is *diatheke*, which is the regular Greek word for "covenant." Translated this way, these verses bring out a fact of great importance concerning the concept of covenant:

> Where a covenant is, there must of necessity be the death of the one who made it. *For a covenant is valid only when men are dead*, for it is never in force while the one who made it lives.
>
> NASB, emphasis added

When you make a covenant, then, you really are signing your own death warrant! It is a solemn affair, the ultimate commitment.

We see the outworking of a covenant relationship in the life of Abraham. The Lord and Abraham had a wonderful, personal relationship. One night the Lord showed Abraham that He would give him the land of Canaan as his inheritance. Abraham asked Him, "How shall I know that I will inherit it?" (Genesis 15:8). God answered Abraham by cutting a covenant with him.

The final commitment of God in any matter, in other words, is a covenant. When God has made a covenant, there is nothing more He needs to do.

In the cutting of this covenant, Abraham was instructed by God to do something customary at that time in the Middle East: to slay certain sacrificial animals, then cut the bodies into two pieces and place the pieces opposite each other with a space in between. Then each party entering into the covenant walked between the pieces. Scripture does not say when Abraham passed between the pieces, but it does describe how God did it:

> It came to pass, when the sun went down and it was dark, that behold, there was a smoking oven and *a burning torch that passed between those pieces.*
>
> Genesis 15:17, emphasis added

In that burning torch the Lord passed through the pieces of the sacrifices. In Hebrews 12:29 we are reminded that "our God is a consuming fire."

What does it mean to pass through the pieces of the sacrifice? It means that once you have passed through the sacrifice and looked at those dead bodies, you say, "That death was my death. From now on I die to myself and live for the one with whom I am in covenant." Abraham renounced his life to live in covenant with God. But bear in mind that God did the same for Abraham.

21

Each party in a covenant can lay claim to whatever the other owns. So it was that later, on the basis of this covenant, the Lord said to Abraham, in effect, "I want your son, Isaac, your only son, the one you love. Offer him to Me as a sacrifice in a place that I will show you" (see Genesis 22:2).

Abraham was a covenant keeper. He neither argued nor delayed. He responded, "All right, God. Here I am. I'll go to the place. I'll offer the sacrifice." And early the next morning he set out for the appointed place.

Right at the last moment, when Abraham had his hand upraised to plunge the knife into the body of his son, the Lord said to him, "All right, Abraham. You don't need to do it. Now I know that you fear Me, since you have not withheld your only son from Me." That is covenant!

But it is not the end of the story. Nearly two thousand years later, the Lord said, "Abraham and his descendants need a sacrifice. There's only one Person who can make that sacrifice—My Son. Abraham offered his son to Me. Now I'm offering My Son for him." That was the other half of the covenant that had been initiated on Mount Moriah. In fulfillment of the covenant commitment into which God the Father had entered there, He offered up His Son, Jesus, at Calvary as the final, all-sufficient sacrifice for sin.

Viewed in that light, history is the outworking of God's covenants with His people. We cannot overemphasize the significance and solemnity of covenant.

Now, apply this to the covenant of marriage. When a Christian man and woman get married, they pass together through the sacrifice of Jesus on the cross. Each one of them says, as Paul said, "I am crucified with Christ: nevertheless I live; yet not I, but Christ liveth in me" (Galatians 2:20, KJV).

After they have made their commitment to one another, each turns back and looks at the cross. The husband says, "When I came through that sacrifice, I died. I laid down my life. Now I live out my life in my mate. She is the expression of my life." The wife says the same: "When I passed through that sacrifice, I died. I no longer live for myself. I'm living now for the one with whom I am in covenant." Each lays down his life or her life for the other. That is the basis of Christian marriage, and the only basis on which a marriage can truly succeed.

This attitude is contrary, however, to that of many people today. That is why so many marriages break up. Too many people today enter marriage wondering, *What will I get out of this?* That does not work. The biblical attitude is, *What will I give?* And that works!

The Purpose of the Marriage Covenant

Adam did not think up marriage. He did not even know he needed a wife. Marriage originated in the mind of God. All the rules for it, as well as its end purpose, were established by Him.

God's purpose for marriage is unity between the partners. But the Bible makes it clear that there is only one basis for true unity between human beings, whether they are men or women: It is covenant. The Bible describes marriage this way:

> Therefore shall a man *leave* his father and his mother, and shall *cleave* unto his wife: and they shall be one flesh.
>
> Genesis 2:24, kjv, emphasis added

The key to marriage is two words: *leave* and *cleave*. If you do not leave, you cannot cleave. If you are not willing to step out of your parental background and make a new start, you will never achieve true unity with your spouse.

In some cultures marriages often do not work, because the culture teaches that the man shall cleave to his father and mother, rather than to his wife. That loyalty stands between him and loyalty to his wife.

It is essential to understand that marriage, as depicted in the Bible, is not a matter of social customs or culture. Many different social customs determine how a marriage is entered into or celebrated. In the land of Israel, for instance, the Jews follow one set of social customs in celebrating a marriage, the Arabs follow another and the Armenians yet another. This is legitimate. But the essential nature of marriage was determined by God Himself at the beginning of human history: A man shall leave his father and mother and shall cleave to his wife. That is the only basis on which a man and a woman can achieve true unity.

Another misunderstanding of marriage is common today. Many people speak and act as if marriage is an experiment. That is a mistake. Marriage is a *commitment*, not an experiment. It is a contradiction in terms to speak about an "experimental commitment." Only through mutual commitment will God release the grace that a man or woman needs to live in unity with his or her marriage partner.

The Prophetic Nature of Marriage

One exciting fact about the God of the Bible is that He delights to reveal Himself to human beings. The revelation of Himself is one of the most precious treasures God offers us. The main channel through which this revelation comes is the Bible. Yet it is an even greater privilege when God chooses to reveal Himself not merely *to* us, but also *through* us.

God often worked in this way through the prophets of the Old Testament. To warn the people of Judah of their impending captivity, God told Jeremiah to put yokes on his own neck (see Jeremiah 27:2). To depict the impending capture of Jerusalem by the Babylonian army, God told Ezekiel to dig through a wall and act like someone escaping from a besieged city (see Ezekiel 12:4–5). To demonstrate God's forgiving love for Israel, God told Hosea to marry a prostitute (see Hosea 1:2). Many similar examples could be given.

So we see that one of the ways we can be prophetic is not merely by speaking a message but by demonstrating it in our actions. Seen in this light, Christian marriage takes on the character of a beautiful prophetic message.

First of all, the personal relationship between a man and his wife demonstrates the bond of unity that only a covenant relationship can produce.

But there is a second and even more wonderful message that a truly Christian marriage conveys. In Ephesians 5:25 Paul says, "Husbands, love your wives, just as Christ also loved the church and gave Himself for it." A Christian husband has the privilege to demonstrate toward his wife the same kind of sacrificial, self-giving love that Christ has for His Church.

On the other side, in Ephesians 5:24, Paul says, "Just as the church is subject to Christ, so let the wives be to their own husbands in everything." A Christian wife has a corresponding privilege to demonstrate in her relationship with her husband the same kind of reverential love that the Church has for Christ her Lord.

Contemporary society has no time for attitudes such as these, which proceed from a life laid down. But this makes it all the more important for Christians in their marriage relationships to represent faithfully the love relationship between Jesus and His Church. At times the testimony of our lives can be more effective than the words of our mouths. Like Old Testament prophets, we can be prophetic not merely by our words but also by our actions.

3

The Role of the Husband

At the beginning of human history God committed to Adam, the first husband, a specific responsibility: "The Lord God took the man and put him in the garden of Eden to tend and keep it" (Genesis 2:15). The English does not convey the full meaning of the word translated "keep." It comes from a word of which the basic meaning is "to guard" or "protect." The modern Hebrew word for "night watchman" is derived from this root. God held Adam responsible to "guard" the Garden. Guard it from what? From the entrance of any "beast of the field" (Genesis 2:20) that had no place in the Garden.

The very next chapter reveals that Adam failed in his responsibility. The serpent, who was a "beast of the field," made his way into the Garden.

Then Adam failed in his next obligation: to protect his wife from Satan's cunning attack. Scripture does not reveal where Adam was at that moment, but it is clear that he left Eve on her own.

At that point Eve added her sin to that of her husband. She entered into conversation with the serpent, succumbed to his deception and ate of the forbidden fruit. She also gave some to her husband, and he ate of it, too.

This reveals that the first two sins in human history were sins of *omission*. Adam failed not in what he did but in what he did not do.

Sins of *omission* then led to sins of *commission*. The third sin was committed by Eve, who was deceived by the serpent and ate of the forbidden fruit. She also involved her husband by giving him some of the fruit to eat. The primary sin of the man was the sin of *omission*; he was delinquent. Then Adam's sin of *omission* opened the way for Eve's sin of *commission*.

People tend to think of sins of omission as less serious than sins of commission. But this is not how Scripture represents them. In Matthew 25:31–46 Jesus gives a prophetic parable concerning the judgment of the "sheep" and "goat" nations at the end of the age. To the goat nations He pronounces one of the most fearsome judgments ever to be uttered: "Depart from Me, you cursed, into the everlasting fire prepared for the devil and his angels" (verse 41).

What did those nations do to incur such a horrific judgment? The answer can be given in one word: *nothing*. They gave no food, no drink, no clothing; they showed no compassion. Yet for those sins of omission they were condemned to everlasting punishment.

The double failure of Adam and Eve set a pattern that has been repeated in every subsequent generation. The primary, characteristic sin of men is a sin of omission, not of commission. They fail in their responsibility—first to their wives, then to their whole families. The characteristic sin of women is to go beyond the limits of their authority and to usurp the functions of men.

27

The aggressive feminist movement is merely the latest in a long series of unhappy consequences of the continuing failure of both men and women. It is important to see, however, that the initial failure of men opens the way for women to move out of their places and usurp the functions of men. The number one problem of Western civilization, in my view, is delinquent men, just as the number one problem of delinquent children is delinquent parents.

The failure of both Adam and Eve marred the perfection of the relationship that God planned for them to have toward each other. Nevertheless their failure did not set aside the basic principle on which God intended their relationship to be built. I call theirs a relationship of *initiative* and *response*. According to this pattern, Adam, as husband, was responsible to take the initiative, and Eve, his wife, was responsible to respond.

Let me illustrate with a down-to-earth example: the act of sexual intercourse. A man may be slow and unresponsive, while the woman may use all her feminine arts. But in the final outcome, unless the man takes the initiative, intercourse will not take place. (This is one reason some feminists adopt a homosexual lifestyle. They refuse to depend on a man's initiative.) I believe the Creator intended this as a pattern to be reproduced in every area of relationship between the sexes: The role of the man is to take the initiative and that of the woman is to respond.

In our contemporary culture, however, there are many other aspects of the relationship between the sexes in which the principle of initiative and response has been set aside. Men have failed in their basic responsibility and women have taken over the male role. The inevitable outcome, whether in a family, nation or civilization, can be summed up in one word: *confusion.*

The Husband's Responsibilities

What are some of the main areas in which a husband should take the initiative? The New Testament suggests six main responsibilities.

1. Love Your Wife

This is not a suggestion or recommendation. It is a command, clearly stated in Ephesians 5:25: "Husbands, love your wives. . . ." To put it simply: If you do not love your wife, you are disobedient to Scripture.

The same verse also tells you the way to love her: ". . . just as Christ also loved the church and gave Himself for it." Notice that this is not a taking love but a giving love—a self-giving love. It is the husband who should take the initiative in giving himself to and for his wife.

Many in our contemporary culture think of love as purely emotional. This is an incomplete picture. Genuine love is released by an act of the will. In Psalm 18:1 David says, "I will love You, O LORD." David made a decision. His love for the Lord was released by an act of his will.

Furthermore the word David uses here for *love* is related to the Hebrew word that can be translated "bowels" or "womb." It was what we call in contemporary speech "a gut feeling." It included both David's will and his emotions. That is the kind of love a husband should have for his wife.

In biblical times most marriages were arranged. The decision of who was to marry whom was made by the parents. This is still true in many parts of the world today. Yet the fact that a marriage was arranged did not mean there would not be warm, deep love between the husband and wife. In fact, countries that practice marriage by arrangement produce a higher ratio of successful marriages than the so-called "free" West, where the divorce rate sometimes approaches fifty percent.

In saying this I am not necessarily advocating arranged marriages. My point is that success in marriage does not depend ultimately on how it was entered into, but on how a husband and wife conduct themselves after they are married. If both are faithful to fulfill their respective responsibilities as assigned to them by Scripture, the marriage will be successful and there will be genuine love between them.

2. Receive Input

The husband should always make room for his wife to speak her mind freely and be sensitive to what she is thinking or feeling, even when she does not express it in words. Her unspoken feelings are often her deepest, and the ones of which her husband needs to be most aware. Communication failure between husband and wife is probably the most common single factor in the breakdown of a marriage.

A husband also needs to remember that his wife has her own special kind of wisdom, often called "intuition." He may work out some conclusion by a laborious process of reasoning, but when he communicates this to his wife, he may be surprised when she responds, "I knew that all along."

3. Make Decisions

Once there has been free and respectful communication between husband and wife, they come to the place where a practical decision has to be made. At this point it is the husband's responsibility to make the final decision. In many cases, if there has been good communication, the wife is happy to let her husband bear this responsibility.

4. Initiate Action

Generally this follows as a logical consequence of the decision making process just outlined. But normally the person responsible for taking the practical steps to carry out a decision is the husband.

The husband may need to delegate many practical daily tasks to his wife, but he should be careful to shoulder a reasonable portion of their shared responsibilities as a couple, especially if they are also parents. And the division of labor could be based, in part, on their spiritual gifting. In addition the wife should be able to count on her husband to be there behind her if she finds herself faced with a crisis she does not know how to handle.

5. Nourish and Cherish

One word should describe the attitude of every husband toward his wife: *special*. Every husband should say to himself, *My wife is special. There's no one else just like her.* For this reason he should relate to her in a way that he relates to no other woman. This does not apply merely to their sexual relationship; it should apply to the way he thinks about her, the way he talks about her, the way he treats her.

In Ephesians 5:28–29 Paul says that a man should love and care for his wife in a particularly personal way:

> Husbands ought to love their own wives as their own bodies; he who loves his wife loves himself. For no one ever hated his own flesh, but nourishes and cherishes it, just as the Lord does the church.

The two words *nourish* and *cherish* suggest an attitude of intimate concern that includes attention to what might appear to be small details. A husband should be concerned about his wife's health, her appearance, the way she does her hair, the perfume she uses. Everything that concerns her should concern him. She should always have the confidence that to her husband she is the most important person in the world.

Let me assure you, husbands: If you sow into your wife in this way, you will reap an abundant harvest!

6. Give Praise

The last part of the last chapter of Proverbs describes and extols the character of the "virtuous," or excellent, wife. It points out her many achievements; then it closes with words of praise:

> Her children rise up and call her blessed; her husband also, and he praises her: "Many daughters have done well, but you excel them all."
>
> Proverbs 31:28–29

Some husbands are stingy with their words of praise. That is false economy! They would be surprised to discover how much a wife longs to be praised—and how she responds to it. Giving praise to your wife is one of the best investments you can ever make.

If a man has a faithful, committed wife, there is no way he can ever offer her in money what she is worth. As Solomon says in this passage, "Her worth is far above rubies" (verse 10). The least a husband can do is offer his wife words of heartfelt praise.

A Final Challenge

An experienced minister was once asked about a certain person, "Is he a good Christian?" The minister replied, "I don't know; I can't tell you yet. I haven't met his wife." That was a wise answer. A husband's success is seen in his wife.

Why not apply this test to yourself as a husband? Perhaps you need to focus less on yourself and more on your wife. Ask yourself—and her as well—the following questions, in order to evaluate how you are doing: *Is she secure and fulfilled? Do I feel proud of her?* If the answers are yes, you are a successful husband.

But if there are obvious areas in your wife's personality that are incomplete, if she shows strain or insecurity, you need to check on your performance as a husband. Perhaps you would do well to read once more through the preceding list of your responsibilities as a husband. Then, if you see you have been delinquent, repent before the Lord and ask Him for the grace you need to do better.

4

The Role of the Wife

The first topic of this book is *husbands,* but any description of the husband's role would be incomplete without at least a brief account of the role of the wife. A marriage operates smoothly only when each partner functions in his or her biblical role. So let's look at what the Bible has to say about the wife.

1. She Is a Helper

> The LORD God said, "It is not good that man should be alone; I will make him a helper comparable to him."
>
> Genesis 2:18

This could be translated, "I will make him a helper to complete him," which would seem to imply that a man without his wife is incomplete. The language in Hebrew is hard to render in English, but let's focus on the main point: God provided the woman to be a *helper.*

Many women today think, *If I'm a helper, I'm inferior.* That is a mistake. In the Body of Christ no one is superior or inferior to anyone else. Each of us is given a place and function. What God requires of us is faithfulness in the particular place and function He has assigned us.

In John 14:16–17 Jesus speaks of the provision He will make for His disciples after He leaves them: "I will pray the Father, and He will give you another *Helper* . . . the Spirit of truth" (emphasis added). So Jesus describes the Holy Spirit as *Helper*, but does that mean the Holy Spirit is inferior? On the contrary, He is God!

In the same way, a wife who fulfills her God-given role as helper is in no way inferior on that account. I thank God that each of my wives has been to me a wonderful helper. I could never have achieved what I have without either Lydia, my first wife, or Ruth, my second.

2. She Submits to Her Husband

This concept has been the subject of controversy in recent years, but the apostle Paul spells it out clearly in Ephesians 5:22:

> Wives, submit to your own husbands, as to the Lord.

Much of the controversy is due to the fact that this verse has been detached from its biblical context. (In fact, in the Bible I have before me at this moment, the editors have actually inserted a subhead dividing verses 21 and 22.) The previous verse is addressed to all Christians: "Submitting to one another in the fear of God." This is the primary submission within the Body of Christ—*all Christians to each other.* This should be the distinctive mark of all Christians: a meek, submissive attitude toward our fellow believers.

Within this context of mutual submission, the wife is granted a unique and special privilege: By her attitude toward her husband, she depicts the attitude of the Church toward Christ. Seen in this context, submission is not a duty imposed on the wife, but a special privilege granted her.

Both Peter, who was married, and Paul, who was unmarried, began their teaching on order in the home with the wife's responsibility to submit to her husband. There is a practical reason for this: If the wife does not fulfill her responsibility, it is almost impossible for the husband to fulfill his. The wife holds the key either to open the door to her husband's fulfillment of his role as head of the family, or else to close it against him. If the wife does not submit willingly to her husband's headship, there is only one way he can take that position—by self-assertive domination. No sensible wife would want that!

What if a wife chooses not to submit and her husband chooses not to take his place as head? Such a family is left unprotected spiritually. It is like a ship on a stormy sea with no captain on the bridge. It is doomed to suffer shipwreck.

The unprotected families in our contemporary culture are the primary cause of the social instability and disorder we are experiencing. There is only one truly effective solution: to restore divine order in our families.

My first wife was considerably older than I was when we were married. Already an experienced missionary, she had succeeded in a difficult field of ministry. She was well educated and a gifted speaker. Had she wished to dominate me, she would have had no trouble doing so! But to her credit she allowed this inexperienced young man to come in and be head of the home.

She must have suffered agonies at some of the things I did! Bear in mind, I had no brothers or sisters, and suddenly found myself head of a house of eight girls. That involved some suffering on the part of all of us!

If Lydia had held onto her place as head of the work, I would have gone through life as "Lydia's husband." But thank God, Lydia let me take my place.

3. She Supports or Upholds

God has so created the human body that the head cannot hold itself up. If the man is the head of the home, it is the body that has to hold him up. And the one primarily responsible is the wife.

We men are weak creatures in many ways. We need support! We can put on a macho exterior and throw our weight around, but inside we are often mice. A spiritual wife will see her husband's weaknesses but not focus on them. Rather she will uphold him, wisely and tactfully, as he struggles to overcome them.

4. She Encourages

There is nothing more painful than a wife who discourages her husband. Imagine a preacher who has just delivered a poor sermon and faced a disappointing response from his congregation. If his wife says on the way home, "That was a terrible sermon!" he can sink no lower; he is a worm! But if she says, "That wasn't one of your best sermons, but I enjoyed it," he begins to think, *Well, maybe there's hope. Maybe I can make it after all.*

I have already pointed out that one title of the Holy Spirit is "the Helper," but that word could just as well be translated "the Encourager." When a wife encourages her husband, she is fulfilling the role of the Holy Spirit in that situation.

5. She Intercedes for Her Husband

Wives sometimes fall into the trap of spending so much time worrying about their husbands, criticizing them and pointing out their faults, that they fail to pray for them. A wife on her knees thanking God for her husband will be the one to reap the benefits.

Ruth and I were associated at one time with two couples who had difficult marriages. In each case there were serious weaknesses and problems in the life of the husband. Those two wives agreed to meet together every morning and intercede for their husbands. They did this faithfully for a number of years. Today each husband is a success, one in Christian ministry, the other in the secular world. Those men would never have become what they are without their wives' persistent, faithful intercession.

Interceding produces better dividends than criticizing or complaining.

My Tribute to Ruth

While I was working on this book, God called my wife Ruth home to Himself. For twenty years she and I enjoyed a happy, fruitful and successful marriage. There were certain reasons for this.

First, we were both committed Christians. For each of us, our primary purpose in life was to serve and glorify the Lord Jesus Christ.

Second, we both believed it was God's plan that we be joined together as husband and wife.

Third, we were both convinced that the New Testament pattern of marriage is still in force today. We never sought to dismiss its requirements as being merely "cultural" or "for another age."

Fourth, Ruth was selfless. She was a capable, talented woman who could have achieved success in her own right. But she believed it was her assignment from God in every way possible to enable me to fulfill my God-given ministry. She was jealous not for her own success but for mine.

I must add, however, that Ruth's commitment to me and my ministry never caused her to be servile or flattering. If she thought I was doing something wrong or was in danger of making a mistake, she would always tell me so frankly. She was particularly concerned that I dress in a way that she considered appropriate to the ministry God had given me. If she felt I was careless in my grooming or attire, she would say, "You look like a man who doesn't have a wife."

During our twenty years of marriage, my ministry expanded in an amazing way. At the time we were married, I was a traveling Bible teacher who had published a few books and had access to a very limited circle in the Body of Christ. By the time God called Ruth home, Derek Prince Ministries was making a global impact. My radio Bible teaching ministry, which began the year after Ruth and I married, was being translated into at least a dozen languages, including Russian, Spanish, Arabic and four dialects of Chinese. I had published at least twenty more books, portions of which have been translated into at least sixty foreign languages. Ruth and I conducted meetings on every continent except Antarctica. Together we made four 'round-the-world ministry trips. Offices of Derek Prince Ministries are now established in at least thirty countries outside the U.S.

My purpose in stating all this, apart from paying a brief tribute to Ruth's memory, is to emphasize one incontrovertible fact: It could never have happened without Ruth's selfless, unfailing, wholehearted support.

Almost every day I used to tell Ruth two things: "You're my sweetheart" and "I think you're wonderful!" I still feel that way.

When the rewards are given out in glory, Ruth will receive her full share. I look forward to being there to see it!

At this point, perhaps, you are asking yourself, *If Derek and Ruth could enjoy such a happy, fruitful marriage, why do so few marriages today seem to achieve that kind of success?*

Well, one common reason is that many couples have failed to include in their marriage one essential ingredient. This will be the theme of my next chapter.

5

The Missing Ingredient

A well-known evangelical minister and his wife were sharing with me frankly some of the struggles they had experienced in making their marriage work. At one point the wife was recounting that their inner tensions had exploded one day into an angry argument in their bedroom.

The husband had been emphasizing—as husbands often do—the scriptural command to wives to be submissive to their husbands. The wife had been emphasizing—as wives often do—that she did not see why she should submit to him. "After all," she told him, "you don't have a good track record. You've made some pretty stupid decisions!"

At this point they both realized they were not acting like Christians. Spontaneously they knelt down on opposite sides of their bed to pray.

"As we did that," the wife recalled to me, "it was as if a cold wind blew through our bedroom. Somehow it impressed on each of our hearts the phrase from Ephesians

5:21, 'submitting to one another *in the fear of God'* (emphasis added). We both recognized there was something missing in our relationship to each other—*the fear of God*. We'd been acting as if our relationship was only on the human level. We had left God out of it."

When they saw this, both repented of their failures and asked forgiveness of God and of each other. That was the beginning of a new relationship between them—a relationship in which they both accepted the place God had allotted to each of them.

That scene in their bedroom, which the wife had described so vividly, kept coming back to me. Gradually I came to see it as a diagnosis explaining why so many marriages between Christians never attain to the standard set forth clearly in the New Testament. They are leaving out one essential ingredient: *the fear of the Lord*.

It so happens that both Lydia and Ruth were excellent cooks—for which I praise God! Both of them were collectors of recipes. In this way I have come to see that in preparing something like a cake or pie, there is often one essential ingredient on which the flavor of the whole recipe depends. Even though all the other ingredients may be there and combined correctly, without this one key ingredient the cake or the pie never tastes the way it should.

There are two versions of the Christmas cake, for instance—one American, the other English. In the English version marzipan, a sweet almond paste, is an essential distinctive ingredient, while an American Christmas cake is usually made without marzipan. For me, with my English background, a cake without marzipan is not a Christmas cake. It is the marzipan that makes the difference.

How does this apply to a Christian marriage? Well, the "marzipan" is the fear of the Lord. Without that distinctive ingredient the marriage is on the same level as one between unbelievers. It can never become what God intends. It will lack that special flavor that should distinguish it from marriages between unbelievers.

Respect, Reverence and Awe

Unfortunately many contemporary Christians have a wrong concept of what the Bible means by *the fear of the Lord*. They disdain it as something outdated that belongs only in the Old Testament and has no place in New Testament Christianity. Nothing could be further from the truth! Actually the fear of the Lord carries a higher priority in the character requirements of the New Testament than in those of the Old.

We need to ask ourselves, therefore: What does the Bible mean by the expression *the fear of the Lord?* It covers three related English words: *respect, reverence* and *awe*. Fearing God is not a cringing, slavish attitude. It is the appropriate response of the creature to the Creator—to His omnipotence, His majesty, His glory and His holiness.

In Psalm 19:9 David says, "The fear of the LORD is clean, *enduring forever*" (emphasis added). The fear of the Lord will never become out of date. It is absolutely pure and absolutely purifying—something that, in all ages, God looks for in His people.

In Isaiah 11:2 the prophet predicted the sevenfold anointing of the Holy Spirit that was to mark Jesus as the promised Messiah, the Anointed One. The seven different aspects of the anointing are: *the Spirit of the Lord* (the Spirit that speaks in the first person as God), *the Spirit of wisdom, the Spirit of understanding, the Spirit of counsel, the Spirit of might, the Spirit of knowledge* and finally (to crown the list) *the Spirit of the fear of the Lord*.

We might have assumed that there was no place for the fear of the Lord in Jesus, God's beloved Son. Yet Isaiah 11:2

reveals the fear of the Lord as the final seal marking Jesus as being truly the Messiah and the Son of God. If Jesus was thus marked by the fear of the Lord, how can we, as His disciples, ever feel that such fear has no place in us?

Recognizing the Cost of Our Redemption

Christians sometimes adopt the attitude that because God in His love has received us and made us His children, there is no place for the fear of the Lord in our lives. Actually the opposite is true. The very fact that God has redeemed us at the infinite cost of His Son's most precious blood should inspire in us an awesome sense of our responsibility to lead lives that give Him the glory that is His due.

In 1 Peter 1:17–19 the apostle declares that the price paid for our redemption should inspire in us a holy fear of failing to lead lives that give God the glory due to Him:

> If you call on the Father, who without partiality judges according to each one's work, conduct yourselves throughout the time of your sojourning here in fear [fear of the Lord]; knowing that you were not redeemed with corruptible things, like silver or gold, from your aimless conduct received by tradition from your fathers, but with the precious blood of Christ, as of a lamb without blemish and without spot.

So far from suggesting that our redemption leaves no place in our lives for the fear of the Lord, Peter emphasizes that it is our only appropriate response!

As I seek to depict in my mind the impact that the fear of the Lord should have in my life, I picture myself standing at the top of a steep, rugged cliff overlooking a rock-strewn valley hundreds of feet below. A guardrail keeps me from venturing too close to the edge. I picture that guardrail as the warnings of Scripture and its demands for holy living. Then I ask myself, *Suppose I were to be presumptuous, climb over the guardrail and take my stand on the very edge of the cliff? After that, just one step more would precipitate me to final, irretrievable disaster!*

As I entertain this thought, the muscles of my stomach tighten up involuntarily and a cold chill runs down my spine. I recall, too, the words of warning written to the Hebrew Christians: "It is a fearful thing to fall into the hands of the living God" (Hebrews 10:31).

This attitude of reverent awe should govern not only our attitude toward God Himself, but also toward His Word, the Scripture. In Isaiah 66:2 the Lord says, "This is the one I esteem: he who is humble and contrite in spirit, and trembles at my word" (NIV).

Why should we tremble at the Scripture? Because this is the way both God the Father and God the Son come into our lives. In John 14:23 Jesus says, "If anyone loves Me, he will keep My word; and My Father will love him, and We [the Father and the Son] will come to him and make Our home with him." Our attitude toward Scripture reveals how much we truly love Jesus and opens the way for God in His fullness to come into our lives. When we read, or hear, the Bible, our attitude should be the same as it would be if God the Father and God the Son were standing in person before us.

A Key to Joy and Fruitfulness

This attitude of reverent awe for God and His Word, contrary to what we might expect, is the key to experiencing the kind of joy that only God can give. In Psalm 2:11 the psalmist exhorts us, "Serve the LORD with fear, and rejoice with trembling."

A beautiful balance is depicted here. We rejoice in God's mercy and at the same time tremble at His awesomeness.

This balance between fear and encouragement was reproduced in the New Testament Church. Acts 9:31 says of the Church in all Judea, Galilee and Samaria that, "walking in the fear of the Lord and in the comfort of the Holy Spirit, they were multiplied." To the natural mind this seems a strange combination—the *fear* of the Lord and the *comfort* of the Holy Spirit. How do fear and comfort go together? Yet this combination was the key to the vibrant life and explosive growth of the New Testament Church.

Probably at this point you are asking yourself, *What does all this about the fear of the Lord have to do with the relationship between husbands and wives?* I would answer in one word: Everything! Out of my own experience in a Christian home, and out of counseling many Christians with problems in their marriages, I have come to a simple conclusion: *Without the fear of the Lord in both husband and wife, a Christian marriage can never become what God intends it to be.*

This is the ingredient on which the flavor of the whole cake depends. Both husband and wife may say all the right things, make all the right resolutions and even attend the best counseling sessions, but without the fear of the Lord as an active force at work in both their lives, their marriage will never become what God intends it to be.

There is only one secure base for this kind of attitude in both husband and wife. In the last resort it all depends on our personal relationship to the Lord Jesus. He graciously invites us into an intimate relationship with Himself, but never at the expense of our consciousness that He is the personal, majestic, awe-inspiring revelation of God the Father. He is our Savior but He is also our Judge, to whom we must all one day give an account. In the New Testament this is vividly illustrated in the account of two of His closest disciples, John and Paul.

At the Last Supper John was so close to Jesus that he could lean on His breast and whisper in His ear. Later, however, when John was suddenly confronted in a vision by the glorious, ascended Christ of God, he said, "I fell at His feet as dead" (Revelation 1:17).

Later Paul, too, enjoyed an ongoing relationship of intimate fellowship with the Lord. Yet he never lost the consciousness that one day he, like every other Christian, would have to give an account of his life to Christ, who would then be seated on His judgment throne. In this context Paul wrote in 2 Corinthians 5:10–11:

> We must all appear before the judgment seat of Christ, that each one may receive the things done in the body, according to what he has done, whether good or bad. Knowing, therefore, the terror of the Lord, we persuade men.

It was Paul's consciousness of the awesome majesty of Christ that made his message persuasive.

When a man regulates his relationship with his wife by the all-pervading fear of the Lord, and when his wife responds in the same spirit, their marriage will fulfill the plan of God unfolded in Scripture. Each will bear in mind the awesome responsibility placed on them. The husband by his conduct toward his wife will make it his aim to depict the attitude of Christ toward His bride, the Church. The wife, on her side, will seek to respond to her husband as the Church responds to Christ, the Bridegroom. Certainly there will be faults and failings on both sides. But these will be covered over as each repents and seeks forgiveness from the other.

Like a cool breeze at the close of a hot and dusty day, the fear of the Lord will temper and dispel the various frustrations and disharmonies inevitable in any marriage. Both husband and wife will find fulfillment in their God-given roles and blend together in the kind of harmony God had in mind when He said, "The two shall become one flesh."

6

The Spiritual Authority of a Harmonious Marriage

A man and his wife living together in true harmony is one of the sweetest blessings God has to offer this side of heaven. Yet it is more than that. It is a door to a realm of spiritual authority that comparatively few Christians ever achieve.

We have already seen the purpose of God in creating a wife for Adam. Now we will go further back and look at God's original purpose in creating mankind:

> God created man in His own image; in the image of God He created him; male and female He created them. Then God blessed them, and God said to them, "Be fruitful and multiply; fill the earth and subdue it; have dominion over the fish of the sea, over the birds of the air, and over every living thing that moves on the earth."
>
> Genesis 1:27–28

God did not give dominion of the earth to Adam alone. He was speaking to both Adam and Eve. It was His intention that the man and woman together should rule the earth on His behalf.

I want to suggest to you that one of the strongest elements in spiritual warfare and in the exercise of authority is a married couple in harmony and unity. It is still God's way to exercise dominion. Not the man on his own, nor the woman on her own, but the man and woman united according to God's pattern in marriage. They have the privilege to exercise dominion on God's behalf.

We understand the vital importance of this when we realize that, as Christians, we are caught up in a life-and-death struggle with invisible evil forces seeking to destroy us. Paul describes this conflict in Ephesians 6:12:

> We do not wrestle against flesh and blood, but against principalities, against powers, against the rulers of the darkness of this age, against spiritual hosts of wickedness in the heavenly places.

Then, in Ephesians 6:18, Paul reveals that our wrestling match is in the arena of prayer: "praying always with all prayer and supplication in the Spirit." It is in this arena that a married couple can become invincible—when they meet one vital condition.

The Prayer of Agreement

In Matthew 18:18–20 Jesus explains how, as Christians, we can become irresistible in our prayer lives:

> "Assuredly, I say to you, whatever you bind on earth will be bound in heaven, and whatever you loose on earth will be loosed in heaven. Again I say to you that if two of you agree on earth concerning anything that they ask, it will be done for them by My Father in heaven. For where two or three are gathered together in My name, I am there in the midst of them."

The minimum number for agreement in such prayer is two or three. With that basic minimum, whatever we bind or loose on earth will be bound or loosed in heaven. Actually, the sense of the Greek verb is "will be having been bound" or "will be having been loosed." So we could say that whatever we bind or loose on earth "will be having been bound or loosed in heaven."

This is exciting because it means that what we say on earth determines what happens in heaven! We may think we are waiting for God to move, which is often true, but there are times when God is waiting for us to move. In a sense the initiative is with us on earth. If we meet the conditions, then whatever we declare on earth is as effective as a decree made in heaven. If we say concerning something on earth, "It is bound," then at that very moment it is bound in heaven. Or if we say on earth, "It is loosed," then at that very moment it is loosed in heaven.

Suppose, for instance, that a Christian couple believe that God is calling them to serve Him in a country that is closed to the Gospel and to all forms of Christian ministry. All their applications for a visa are refused, with no indication that they may apply again later.

Then the Holy Spirit directs them to the picture of Jesus as the One "who has the key of David, He who opens and no one shuts, and shuts and no one opens" (Revelation 3:7). They commit themselves to pray together in agreement, to "bind" the spiritual forces that oppose all Christian witness in the country of their calling and to "loose" the visas they require.

In the months that follow, each of them goes through a process of dying to self. The husband refuses an attractive job promotion because it demands a commitment that would make it impossible to travel outside the United States. The wife agrees to move to a smaller and less convenient home, so they may save money for the expense of moving to the country to which they feel called. After many long months all hope of answering God's call seems lost but, like Abraham, who "contrary to hope, in hope believed" (Romans 4:18), they continue to pray.

Then, quite suddenly, the husband receives a job offer to take over the management of a business in the very country to which God has called them! The door that was closed to him as a Christian minister has now been opened wide to him as the representative of a business that can boost the economy of the country of their calling.

This story, although a composite made up of the experiences of more than one Christian couple, illustrates the effectiveness of the prayer of agreement.

But first, of course, we must meet the conditions. They are twofold.

In the first place our focus must be on Jesus Himself. In Matthew 18:20 the Greek says literally, "Where two or three are gathered together *into* My name. . . ." Jesus Himself must be our focus. The basis of our unity cannot be merely a doctrine or denomination. It must be the Person and work of Jesus Himself.

Again the Greek word translated *agree* in Matthew 18:19 is *sumphoneo*, from which we get the English word *symphony*. Jesus is not speaking of doctrinal or intellectual agreement. He has in mind something both deeper and higher: *spiritual harmony*. This requires two or more people so united in spirit that they think and talk and pray as one person.

As we have seen, the promises Jesus offers to two or more who can achieve this kind of harmony are astonishing: "Whatever you bind on earth will be having been bound in heaven." Again: "If two harmonize on earth concerning anything that they ask, it will be done for them by My Father in heaven." These are truly amazing promises and signify, as I said, that what we say on earth actually determines what happens in heaven.

You might ask, "How can that be?" Let me offer you my understanding. The only Person who can bring two people together in perfect harmony is the Holy Spirit, and He can do this only for those fully yielded to Him. The fact that two can achieve such harmony is evidence, therefore, that they are fully yielded to the Holy Spirit. This means they are praying in harmony not only with each other but also with God. On this basis God commits Himself to hear and answer their prayers.

True harmony is not easy to achieve. You know the painful sound of two singers who are almost—but not exactly—in harmony with each other. The sound they produce grates on the ear. How about married couples who are almost—but not exactly—in harmony when they pray? How do they sound in God's ears? God patiently endures such prayers but He does not commit Himself to respond.

The key to spiritual authority in prayer is harmony between those who are praying. There may be more than two persons or there may be two believers who are not married. Nevertheless the challenge to pray together in harmony is one that uniquely confronts Christian couples.

At a time when Ruth and I were under great pressure, a dear senior brother—a mature servant of God—said to us, "I'm convinced that the key to the success of your ministry is your harmony. Don't let anything spoil it!"

It is never easy to achieve such harmony. There is a price to pay. Harmony can come only to those ready to lay down their lives for the Lord and for each other.

The old carnal nature can never achieve true harmony, not even within itself. There is only one remedy: That old nature must be put to death. But thank God, the death took place nearly two thousand years ago when Jesus died on the cross! "Our old man was crucified with Him," Paul wrote in Romans 6:6. "Likewise," he continued in verse 11, we must now "reckon [ourselves] to be dead indeed to sin, but alive to God in Christ Jesus our Lord."

The Decision Is Yours

The necessity of the death of the carnal nature confronts each of us with a personal decision: *Am I willing to die to myself? Am I ready to come to the place where I can truthfully apply to myself the words of Paul in Galatians 2:20?*

I have been crucified with Christ; it is no longer I who live, but Christ lives in me; and the life which I now live in the flesh I live by faith in the Son of God, who loved me and gave Himself for me.

Understood in this way, the cross becomes the door that makes possible a life of true harmony between husband and wife. After all, Christ living in the husband will never be out of harmony with Christ living in the wife.

Furthermore the cross opens the way to a realm of spiritual authority in prayer that would otherwise seem altogether impossible: "If two of you agree [harmonize] on earth concerning anything that they ask, it will be done for them by My Father in heaven." God will never reject a prayer that is prayed out of true harmony.

But there is only one door to this kind of harmony, either in marriage or in any other personal relationship. It is the cross!

PART 3

Fathers

7

The Ultimate Revelation of God

The fact behind all other facts is that God created the universe as a Father. He left His Father imprint on every aspect of creation.

The apostle Paul wrote: "I bow my knees to the Father of our Lord Jesus Christ, from whom the whole family in heaven and earth is named" (Ephesians 3:14–15). The word here translated "family" is *patria*, which is derived from *pater*, the Greek word for *father*. So the most straightforward translation would be: "I bow my knees to the Father, from whom every *fatherhood* in heaven and earth derives its name."

What a remarkable fact! All fatherhood in the universe did not begin on earth, nor did it begin with time or human history. It began in heaven. Ultimately it goes back to the Fatherhood of God.

Eternally God is the Father of our Lord Jesus Christ; He is described as such in many parts of the Bible. The intimate, personal relationship between the Father and His Son existed before creation ever began. John 1:1 says, "In the beginning [before all time] was the Word [Jesus], and the Word was with God." This fact reveals something unique and special about the nature of God. In God there is not only Fatherhood but also relationship.

1 John 4:16 reveals another fact about God's eternal nature: "God is love." If we put this fact together with that of God's Fatherhood, we arrive at a most wonderful conclusion: *God as a Father created the universe in love. In countless ways the universe He created is the expression and outworking of His Fatherly love.*

All Creation Responds to the Father

Everything God has created responds in its own appropriate way to His love. The heavenly bodies move in harmony with their Creator: "The moon marks off the seasons, and the sun knows when to go down" (Psalm 104:19, NIV). The stars answer to their names when God calls them: "He counts the number of the stars; He calls them all by name" (Psalm 147:4). Isn't it exciting to think that each one of the billions of stars in the universe is known individually to God by its name?

No matter how turbulent the elements appear at times, they always obey their Creator—"fire and hail, snow and clouds; stormy wind, fulfilling His word" (Psalm 148:8).

The same is true of the animal creation: "The young lions roar after their prey, and seek their food from God" (Psalm 104:21). And the psalmist describes "this great and wide sea, in which are innumerable teeming things, living things both small and great. . . . These all wait for You, that You may give them their food in due season" (Psalm 104:25, 27).

Concerning the birds Jesus tells us, "Your heavenly Father feeds them" (Matthew 6:26). In Matthew 10:29 He says, "Are not two sparrows sold for a copper coin? And not one of them falls to the ground apart from your Father's will [or apart from your Father]." And in Luke 12:6 Jesus says, "Are not five sparrows sold for two copper coins? And not one of them is forgotten before God."

So two sparrows are sold for one copper coin, but five sparrows are sold for two copper coins. In other words, if you buy four sparrows, you get a fifth sparrow free. Yet God is concerned about even that fifth sparrow.

There is nothing God has created, in fact, with which He is not intimately concerned. His Fatherly love extends to every creature in the universe, to everything He has created.

The nineteenth-century evangelist Dwight Moody gave the following account of how the world appeared to him after he received Christ as his Savior:

> I remember the morning on which I came out of my room after I had first trusted Christ. I thought the old sun shone a good deal brighter than it ever had before—I thought that it was just smiling upon me; and as I walked out upon Boston Common and heard the birds singing in the trees I thought they were all singing a song to me. Do you know, I fell in love with the birds. I had never cared for them before. It seemed to me that I was in love with all creation.

The great Creator had become Moody's Father, and He gave His newborn son a glimpse of how He Himself viewed the world He had created. All of creation, as Moody saw it, was bathed in the fathomless love of its Creator.

There are only two classes of God's creatures that are alienated and unresponsive to God's love: Satan and his rebellious angels; and fallen, sinful humanity. Satan and his angels rebelled beyond any possibility of reconciliation. It was, however, to reconcile fallen man to Himself that God sent Jesus.

How Jesus Manifested the Father

Jesus was sent by the Father to accomplish two purposes: the first negative, the second positive. The negative purpose was to pay the penalty for our sins, that we might be forgiven and reconciled to God. The positive purpose was to reveal God as our Father and to make us members of His family.

In many sections of the Church, great emphasis has been placed on the first, "negative" purpose of Jesus' coming: to atone for our sins and to reconcile us to God. It is right that this purpose be emphasized; it is the essential first step. But this emphasis should never be at the expense of the second purpose: to reveal God as Father and to make us members of His family.

In John 17 Jesus prayed what has been called His High Priestly prayer on behalf of His disciples. It was, in fact, His last personal communication with them before His arrest, trial and crucifixion. Both at the beginning and at the end of the prayer, Jesus spoke of having made God's name known to His disciples:

"I have manifested Your name to the men whom You have given Me out of the world."

John 17:6

"And I have declared to them Your name, and will declare it, that the love with which You loved Me may be in them, and I in them."

verse 26

What was the name Jesus made known to His disciples? It was not the sacred name *Jehovah* (or "Yahweh"). The Jewish people had known that name for fourteen centuries. It was a new name—a name hinted at in the Old Testament but never openly revealed. That name was *Father*. Jesus described God as Father six times in this prayer, and said, "I have *manifested* Your name. . . ."

Webster defines *manifest* as "to make evident or certain by showing or displaying." Jesus did not merely offer His disciples a theological definition of God; He *manifested* God as Father by the way He lived out His life before them—a life of unbroken fellowship with and total dependence on God. They had never seen anyone live a life like that.

In John 14:6, speaking of His purpose in coming to earth, Jesus said: "I am the way, the truth, and the life. . . ." These words suggest a question: If Jesus is the way, where is He the way *to?* A way is never complete by itself; it presupposes a destination. What, then, is the destination? The closing words of the verse tell us: ". . . No one comes to the Father except through Me."

We talk a great deal about the Lord Jesus Christ as our Savior, our Intercessor, our Mediator and so on. All this is wonderful, but it stops short of Jesus' ultimate purpose: *to bring us to the Father*.

In this respect there is an important difference between the revelation God gave through the prophets in the Old Testament and the revelation He gave through Jesus in the New Testament. In Hebrews 1:1–2 the writer says: "God, who at various times and in different ways spoke in time past to the fathers by the prophets, has in these last days spoken to us by His Son. . . ." More literally, however, these last words should be translated that God "has in these last days spoken to us *in a* Son. . . ."

The point the writer is making is that God did not merely add to the message of the Old Testament prophets by the ministry of Jesus. More than that, the writer reveals that Jesus was *a different kind of messenger*. He was not merely a prophet; He was also a *Son*. He brought a revelation, therefore, that had never been given before, a revelation that only a Son could bring: *a revelation of the Father*.

In Matthew 11:27 Jesus Himself emphasizes that He is the only Person who can bring the revelation of God as Father:

> "All things have been delivered to Me by My Father, and no one knows the Son except the Father. Nor does anyone know the Father except the Son, and he to whom the Son wills to reveal Him."

The Benefits of Knowing the Father

When we come into the fullness of the revelation of God as Father, it supplies five benefits that the majority of people, including many Christians, conspicuously lack.

1. Identity

Modern man has a real problem with identity. It is significant that one of the most successful books and television series in the United States in the 1970s was *Roots*, the story of an African-American looking for the place he had come from.

Both Scripture and psychology agree that a person cannot fully answer the question "Who am I?" without knowing who his or her father is. Because relationships between parents and children have so broken down in the last two generations, our contemporary society is suffering an identity crisis. Multitudes are rootless; they have no sense of belonging.

Christianity's answer to that identity crisis is to bring men and women into a direct, personal relationship with God the Father through Jesus Christ the Son. People who truly know God as Father no longer have an identity problem. They know who they are: They are children of God. Their Father created the universe, their Father loves them and their Father cares for them. They belong to the best family in the universe!

2. Self-Worth

I cannot count how many people I have talked with whose great problem was not appreciating themselves sufficiently. They had too low a picture of themselves, which caused them many spiritual and emotional agonies. When I counsel these people, one passage of Scripture I direct them to is 1 John 3:1: "See how great a love the Father has bestowed on us, that we would be called children of God; and such we are" (NASB).

Once we really comprehend that we are the children of God, that God loves us intimately and personally, that He is interested in us, that He is never too busy for us and that He desires a direct and personal relationship with us, then we discover our self-worth. I have seen this transformation take place in many people's lives.

3. Awareness of a Home in Heaven

Ever since I was saved, I believed that if I continued faithful to the Lord, I would go to heaven when I died. But I never really thought of heaven as my home. Then in 1996 I received a sovereign visitation from God through which I came to know Him, in a direct and personal way, as my Father. Ever since then it has become natural for me to view heaven as my home. Shortly afterward I said to Ruth,

"When I die, if you want to give me a tombstone, you can just write on it two words: *Gone home.*"

I began to think about the poor beggar who lay outside the rich man's door. When he died he was "carried by the angels to Abraham's bosom" (Luke 16:22). Surely one angel would have been sufficient to carry that emaciated form, but God sent an escort of angels! The beggar was given a royal welcome into Abraham's bosom. It should be like that, I believe, for every child of God. The Lord has an escort of angels ready to carry each of us to our eternal home.

At one time Ruth and I came to know a precious Hawaiian sister (we will call her Mary) who served the Lord faithfully for many years. She used to say to her friends, "I've never seen an angel. I would love to see one!"

As Mary lay dying of cancer, her church saw to it that there was always a Christian sister by her bed. One day Mary's face became radiant with the glory of God. She stretched out her arms and said, "I see them—I see the angels!" Then she was gone. Her angelic escort had carried her home.

John Wesley once received word that a Methodist sister he knew had died. He responded, "Did she go in glory, or only in peace?" I believe that God has an escort of angels ready to carry every one of His children home to Him in glory.

4. Total Security

What do we view as the origin of the universe? A big bang? Well, if so, who knows what kind of bang might come next and blot us all out! Is the "bang" just some inanimate force that operates relentlessly without purpose or feeling? Or is it a Father?

You will be a different person the moment you grasp the fact that behind all life is the Fatherhood of God.

A friend of mine was once feeling lost and lonely late at night in the deserted, windy streets of a large city. He was not quite sure that he knew the way back to the place where he was spending the night. As he stood on a street corner, he began to say over and over again, "Father . . . Father . . . Father . . . Father. . . ."

As he did so, security came to him. Even though things were cold and bleak around him, he knew he was a child of God in the universe God has created for His children. And he made it safely back to his quarters.

Picture a child held securely in his father's arms with his little face pressed against his dad's shoulder. There may be confusion and distress all around. The world may seem to be falling apart. But the child is at peace, unconcerned by what is taking place all around him. He is secure in his father's arms.

We, too, are held securely in the arms of our Father. Jesus has assured us that the Father is greater than all that surrounds us, and that no one is able to snatch us out of His hand.

To His disciples Jesus also gave this assurance: "Do not fear, little flock, for it is your Father's good pleasure to give you the kingdom" (Luke 12:32). We may be just a little flock, surrounded by wild beasts of all kinds. But if our Father has committed Himself to give us the Kingdom, no power in the universe can withhold it from us!

5. Motivation for Service

In Philippians 2:3 Paul warns us as servants of the Lord: "Let nothing be done through selfish ambition or conceit. . . ." Over the years I have observed that one persistent, pervasive problem in the Church is the personal ambition of those in ministry, manifesting itself in competition with other ministers. Let me add that I observed this first and foremost in my own life.

We often make the mistake of equating *security* with *success*. If I build the biggest church, or hold the largest meeting, or get the most names on my mailing list, I will be secure. That is a delusion. The fact is, the more we aim at personal success, the less secure we become. We are threatened continually by the possibility that someone else may build a bigger church, or hold a larger meeting, or get more names on his mailing list.

As for me, I have found my perfect pattern in Jesus, who said, "The Father has not left Me alone, *for I always do those things that please Him*" (John 8:29, emphasis added).

I am motivated less and less by personal ambition. I have discovered a sweeter, purer motive: *simply to please my Father*. I am training myself to approach every situation and decision with a single, simple question: *How can I please my Father?* In times of frustration or seeming failure, I seek to turn my focus from trying to solve the problem to maintaining an attitude that is pleasing to the Lord.

As servants of Christ, we will experience no competition among ourselves if we are motivated by this simple desire to please our Father. Harmony and mutual concern take the place of striving and self-seeking.

All this—and more!—is made available to us through the knowledge of God as our Father. If we have found Jesus as the Way, let us rejoice. But let's not be content to continue forever on the way without arriving at the destination: knowing God as Father. To miss this would be to frustrate the very purpose of God in sending Jesus.

The revelation of God as our heavenly Father naturally leads us on to our next theme: How may human fathers represent the Fatherhood of God in their homes?

8

The Father as Priest

God does not just write true statements on pages; He puts truth into persons. We have the Bible and we thank God for the written Scripture. But Jesus said, "I am the truth." Many of us would acknowledge that mere abstract truth will never satisfy us. What satisfies us is the truth in a person. We need to relate not just to an abstraction but to a person.

When I was a professional philosopher, I was wrapped up in all sorts of exciting theories about life and its purpose and Plato's "ideal state." The problem was, I could not live in that rarefied atmosphere all the time. About half the week I was up there with the "theory of ideas," and the other half of the week I was down on earth living in a very carnal way. I was never satisfied, because mere abstract truth never fully satisfies us. When I met Jesus, however, I knew I had met the truth in a Person. That satisfied me as no abstract truth could ever do.

In a certain sense God has committed to every father the responsibility to embody, as a person, the ultimate revelation of the Bible, *fatherhood*. To be a real father is the most perfect depiction of God that any man can achieve, because it is the ultimate revelation of God Himself. In fact, every father represents God to his family. That is not an option! The question is, *Do you as a father represent God rightly or wrongly?*

The greatest curse of our present age is fathers who have misrepresented God. I remember hearing about a man witnessing for Christ on the street to young men and women. He said to one young man, "God wants to be your Father." The youth answered, "My father is the man I hate most in life." Instead of his father being a recommendation, he was a barrier! We all know of fathers like this.

Let's go a step further in the picture of what it is to be a father:

> I want you to know that the head of every man is Christ, the head of woman [or *wife*] is man [or *husband*], and the head of Christ is God.
>
> 1 Corinthians 11:3

This descending chain of authority may be represented by the following simple diagram:

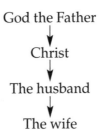

In this chain we find two persons who relate both upward and downward. Christ relates upward to the Father and downward to the man. The man relates upward to Christ and downward to his wife—and, by implication, to his family.

In the same way that Christ represents God to the man, then, the man is responsible to represent Christ to his family. That is quite a job description for a father!

There are, I believe, three main ministries of Christ in which the father should represent Him to his family: priest, prophet and king. In this and the next two chapters, we will look at each of these in turn.

A father's success as priest will determine his success as prophet and king. If he succeeds as priest, he will probably succeed in the other two ministries. But if he does not understand how to be the priest of his family, it will be difficult for him to be either the prophet or the king.

Let's establish, first of all, that the one unique word connected with priesthood is *sacrifice*. According to the biblical pattern, only a priest may offer a sacrifice. So the father, as priest, has the sacred duty of offering sacrifices on behalf of his family.

The following are four main ways in which a father may offer sacrifice on behalf of his family:

1. Offering thanksgiving
2. Making intercession
3. Making the way for salvation
4. Exercising faith for his children

1. Offering Thanksgiving

Our primary ministry as priests in the New Testament is described in Hebrews 13:15:

> Therefore by Him [Jesus] let us continually offer the sacrifice of praise to God, that is, the fruit of our lips, giving thanks to His name.

An alternative translation for the fruit of lips "giving thanks to His name" refers to the fruit of lips that "confess his name" (NIV). The climax of the priestly blessing that Aaron and his descendants were instructed to pronounce on the people of Israel came with these words: "So they shall put My name on the children of Israel, and I will bless them" (Numbers 6:27).

Often the most effective prayers we can offer on behalf of others are prayers of praise and thanksgiving, invoking the name of the Lord Jesus on them. When we put the name of Jesus on those for whom we are praying, we invoke God's blessing on them.

Few of us realize how much we uplift people in their spirits when we simply praise God for them. This is a major part of our ministry as intercessors.

You may have heard of a man known as "Praying Hyde." He was an outstanding missionary in the Punjab in India in the last century when India was still under British rule. Hyde's ministry was prayer; everything else was secondary.

Early on he came across an Indian evangelist whom he considered ineffective and cold. As he began to pray about this man, he said, "Lord, You know how—"

He was going to say, "—how cold Brother So-and-So is." But the Holy Spirit stopped him with Proverbs 30:10: *Don't accuse God's servant to his Master.*

So Brother Hyde changed his approach. He began to think of everything good in that man's life and to thank God for him. Within a few months that man became outstandingly successful as an evangelist.

What changed him? Not being accused in prayer, but being the object of thanksgiving.

I would say to husbands and fathers: Take much more time thanking God for your family, because in so doing you create an atmosphere around them that makes it easy for them to succeed.

There has been a popular bumper sticker on cars in the United States: *Have you hugged your kid today?* That is an important question. But no less important is: *Have you thanked God for your child today?*

God has taught me this: If I cannot thank Him for somebody, I probably have no right to pray for them. I had better not pray at all, because my prayer may do more harm than good.

2. Making Intercession

Let's look at a picture of a man in the Old Testament, Job, who was a model as priest of his family. We read at the opening of the book that Job was a perfect and upright man before God. One day each week his seven sons and three daughters met in the house of one of his sons for feasting and fellowship. At the end of each week Job got up early in the morning and offered sacrifices on behalf of all his children, saying, "It may be that they have failed and are not right with God. I will make a sacrifice on their behalf."

When Job offered a sacrifice for his children, he was claiming the benefits of the sacrifice on their behalf. That is a picture of intercession: claiming the benefits of a sacrifice on behalf of those for whom you are praying.

Our sacrifice at this point in history, of course, is the sacrifice of Jesus on the cross. Intercession for our children, then, involves claiming the benefits of Christ's death on their behalf.

At this point a cynic might comment, "Well, it didn't do much good in Job's case!" It is true that in one disaster all his children were wiped out. But this is one time when we need to read all that the Bible has to say.

After Job had learned his hard lessons, he was gloriously restored—but not until he had prayed for his critics (see Job 42:8–10). Here is a lesson for all of us: We must not let our critics get us down. Rather we should make their

71

charges against us a ladder on which we climb upward. When we pray for them, God will release His grace to us. Look at the details of Job's restoration.

> The LORD blessed the latter days of Job more than his beginning; for he had fourteen thousand sheep, six thousand camels, one thousand yoke of oxen, and one thousand female donkeys. He also had seven sons and three daughters.
>
> Job 42:12–13

Job received exactly double the number of livestock that he had before, but he got only the same number of sons and daughters. Why did God not double them also? My understanding is that Job's prayers had been answered. Though his first set of children had been carried out of time into eternity, they were in God's keeping in the place of the righteous dead awaiting the redemption to come through Jesus Christ. So when God gave Job only ten more children, He was, in fact, giving him double, because the first ten had merely gone ahead and would be waiting for their father when he passed into eternity.

So Job's intercession did pay! In fact, it shows how urgent it was for him to pray for his family. That godly man had no idea that a disaster was coming in which all his children would be carried off in one moment. After the disaster it would have been too late to pray. But Job had prayed already.

Every father, as priest of his family, needs to learn a lesson from Job. None of us has any guarantee that some unforeseen tragedy or disaster will not, in one instant, carry one or more of the members of our family out of time into eternity. Every father is responsible before God, therefore, to maintain day-by-day intercession for his whole household.

We must also guard against the mistake of looking for the answers to our prayers only on earth and in the present age. Only in eternity shall we know the full outworking of our prayers.

3. Making the Way for Salvation

In the ordinances of the Passover, we see a tremendous example of a father's ministry as priest. It was through the sacrifice of the Passover lamb, you will recall, that Israel was delivered out of her slavery in Egypt and brought out to become a new nation. The Egyptians, who had no sacrifice, endured the judgment of God on their firstborn.

The ordinance of the Passover depended on the father. No one else could do what he had to do. Each father was responsible to provide the sacrifice for his household, as the Lord told Moses:

> "Speak to all the congregation of Israel, saying: 'On the tenth day of this month every man shall take for himself a lamb, according to the house of his father, a lamb for a household.'"
>
> Exodus 12:3

In order for the sacrifice to be effective, the father also had to take another step. Moses told the people:

> "And you [that is, every father] shall take a bunch of hyssop, dip it in the blood that is in the basin, and strike the lintel and the two doorposts with the blood that is in the basin. And none of you shall go out of the door of his house until morning. For the LORD will pass through to strike the Egyptians; and when He sees the blood on the lintel and on the two doorposts, the LORD will pass over the door and not allow the destroyer to come into your houses to strike you."
>
> Exodus 12:22–23

73

Who was responsible to select the lamb? The father of every family. Who was responsible to slay the lamb? The father. Who was responsible to sprinkle its blood on the doorposts of the house? The father.

In other words, the father had a God-appointed ministry as priest on behalf of his family. It was his responsibility to see that God's provision of salvation was made effective in his home.

For us today there is a different sacrifice, but the father's responsibility is the same.

4. Exercising Faith for His Children

The dramatic incident of the epileptic boy in Mark 9 gives us many lessons on faith. The disciples could not heal the boy, so the father brought him to Jesus. After hearing the father tell about all the sufferings of the boy, Jesus replied:

> "If you can believe, all things are possible to him who believes." Immediately the father of the child cried out and said with tears, "Lord, I believe; help my unbelief!"
>
> Mark 9:23–24

What impresses me about this story is that the boy could not believe for himself, but that the Lord held the father accountable to believe for his son. This, I believe, is a principle: God holds fathers accountable to have faith for their children.

One principle from the ministry of Jesus became very real to me when God plunged me into the ministry of deliverance. Often people came to the front of a meeting with a child and said, "Pray for him," or, "Pray for her." I learned to ask, "Are you the parents of the child?" Often the answer would be, "No, we're not the parents. The parents are not believers, but we want to bring this child for prayer."

I challenge you to search the ministry of Jesus. He never prayed for a child except on the basis of the faith of one or both parents. His ministry provides no precedent, then, for praying for a child without the participation of at least one parent. Parents have a much greater responsibility than many of us are willing to acknowledge.

What about a child whose parents are not believers? God in His sovereignty can give special faith to people who have no blood relationship with a child. In fact, I can recall cases in my own ministry when He has done this.

The point I want to emphasize, however, is positive and not negative: *Parents have a God-given responsibility to exercise faith on behalf of their children.*

Let me summarize the four main responsibilities of the father as priest of his family:

1. Offering thanksgiving
2. Making intercession
3. Making the way for salvation
4. Exercising faith for his children

In the next chapter I will deal with the second main responsibility of the father: to minister as a prophet to his family.

9

The Father as Prophet

Let's look now at the father's responsibility as prophet of his family.

The difference between the roles of priest and prophet is this: As priest you represent your family to God; as prophet you represent God to your family. Remember, too, that you can be prophetic not merely by what you say but by how you behave. There are four specific ways we fathers can do this.

1. Representing God by Example

A father represents God to his family by example. It is the most Godlike thing a man can do. There is, however, another side to this: A father may represent God to his family, but he may also *misrepresent* God to his family.

Is the father loving, accessible, compassionate, strong? It is easy for a child to picture God this way if that is how his daddy is. But if the father is bitter, angry, critical or just absentee and irresponsible, that child begins life with a negative idea about God. Often it takes a great deal to break down that early misapprehension.

I mentioned earlier the young man who said, "My father is the man I hate most in life." Obviously his father had totally misrepresented God to him.

How does a father function as prophet to his family for good and not for evil? First and foremost, by *love*. Every child is born into this world with an innate longing for love. The love of a mother is beautiful and irreplaceable, but it is not enough. There is a different quality to the love of a father. Even to an infant it imparts a sense of strength, of security, of being important, of being valuable.

When this kind of love is lacking in a child's life, the result is a deep inner wound, probably best described as *rejection*—a sense of being unimportant and unwanted. This was the ultimate wound that killed Jesus on the cross: rejection by His Father. He cried out, "My God, My God, why have You forsaken Me?" (Mark 15:34), but received no answer. Then He bowed His head and breathed His last.

This was the final, terrible consequence Jesus endured because He became identified with the sin of all humanity. So terrible is the evil of sin that God the Father had to close His ears even to the cry of His beloved Son. But remember, Jesus endured our rejection that we might have His acceptance.

Uncounted millions in our contemporary society carry inner wounds of rejection. Some have never known the love of either father or mother. Others have known the love of a mother but not of a father. In most cases this wound of rejection is never actually diagnosed. Those who bear it go through life with a sense of being incomplete, but they never understand just what is missing.

The symptoms of this wound may be either passive or active. On the passive side the symptoms may take any or all of the following forms: *depression, cynicism, lack of motivation, hopelessness* and, ultimately, *suicidal tendencies*. On the active side they may take the form of *frustration, anger, rejection of authority, violence, criminality* and, ultimately, *murder*. The undiagnosed cause of much of the crime and violence in Western society is, in my view, as simple and radical as this: the failure of fathers to love their children.

Sometimes the problem is not that fathers do not love their children, but that they do not know how to demonstrate their love. Undemonstrated love does not meet a child's need.

As I grew up, I was in many ways well cared for. But the people in my family were part of the British society of the "stiff upper lip." They seldom displayed any emotional warmth. It was not that they did not have it in their hearts, but that they were restrained by unwritten social rules from expressing it. I do not recall, for instance, that my father ever took me on his knee. This left a gap in my personality that has been filled only gradually as I have come into a deeper relationship with God as my Father.

I have discovered, however, that God's Fatherly love is neither weak nor sentimental. He does not indulge the moods or fancies of His children. On the contrary His love is expressed by firm discipline: "The Lord disciplines those he loves, and he punishes everyone he accepts as a son" (Hebrews 12:6, NIV).

Throughout the book of Proverbs, Solomon emphasizes both the importance and the urgency of a father's discipline. For instance: "He who spares the rod hates his son, but he who loves him is careful to discipline him" (Proverbs

13:24, NIV). And again: "Discipline your son, and he will give you peace; he will bring delight to your soul" (Proverbs 29:17, NIV).

Experience confirms the soundness of Solomon's counsel. In a house where children are not disciplined, there can be very little peace.

Since the father is head of the family, all discipline should be seen as proceeding from him. At times, however, the mother may be the one who actually carries it out. It is important that parental discipline be consistent. Both parents should follow a pattern of discipline that is mutually agreed upon. Otherwise it is likely that the children will seek to play one parent off against the other.

When exercising discipline, guard against two opposite dangers. The first danger is rebelliousness in the child. To avoid rebellion, make sure your discipline is firm and consistent. Do not allow children to become wayward or irresponsible or to answer you rudely. Require them to do what they are told promptly and quietly.

You must also guard, however, against the opposite extreme, which is discouragement. If a father is unduly severe, critical and demanding, the child will become discouraged and take the attitude, "It's no good. Nothing I do ever pleases Dad. I might as well not even try."

Paul says two things about this: "Fathers, do not exasperate your children, so that they will not lose heart" (Colossians 3:21, NASB) and "Fathers, do not provoke your children to anger" (Ephesians 6:4, NASB).

I have ministered to many people who had severe emotional problems. I cannot estimate how many times a person's lack of self-worth or feeling of failure went back to an incident in childhood when he or she received negative treatment from a parent. It may have been criticism, being made fun of, being scolded unfairly in front of others—or worse. That treatment left a wound in the child's soul that had not healed for maybe twenty or thirty years.

As a father, you must maintain discipline on the one hand, but not discourage your child on the other hand with unfair or excessive demands.

2. Representing God through Teaching

The exercise of discipline in the home will prepare the way for the second facet of your serving as prophet to your family: instructing them in the ways and Word of God.

One of the things that became clear to me as principal of the teacher training college in Kenya is that if you cannot discipline pupils, you cannot teach them. That is why there are so many untaught children in contemporary culture. If you maintain discipline, on the other hand, you can also teach.

Paul says, "And you, fathers, do not provoke your children to wrath, but bring them up in the training and admonition of the Lord" (Ephesians 6:4). Who, according to this verse, is primarily responsible to teach the children the truth of God's Word? The father. But who often does it? The mother. Is that God's order? No. But if that is the way God's Word is taught, when little Johnny is about twelve years old, he may say, "I want to be a man like my dad. He doesn't go to church and he doesn't read the Bible, so I don't have to, either." That is one reason the women in some congregations outnumber the men two to one!

God bless the women who must give the instruction to their families because the father has failed! The problem is, boys get the impression that Christianity is something for women. Women who have the task of instructing their sons, then, need to make sure there is a male spiritual leader somewhere in their boys' lives.

Moses gives some amazingly wise advice to fathers about spiritual instruction in their homes: "You [fathers] shall lay up these words of mine in your heart and in your soul, and bind them as a sign on your hand, and they shall be as frontlets between your eyes" (Deuteronomy 11:18). The Word of God, in other words, should be conspicuous in your life!

In this verse from Deuteronomy 11, I have inserted the word *fathers* in brackets. This is to bring out a point in the original Hebrew that is not made clear in an English translation. Hebrew verbs and pronouns use different forms according to whether the person speaking or the person addressed is masculine or feminine. In the passage quoted above, all the words are in the masculine form. In other words Moses is addressing his remarks primarily—but not exclusively—to the fathers. This does not mean that mothers should have no part in teaching their children. But it means that the father in each family should be seen as the authority from which the teaching proceeds.

In Deuteronomy 11:19 Moses continues: "You shall teach them to your children, speaking of them when you sit in your house, when you walk by the way, when you lie down, and when you rise up."

Every situation in a family's life can be an occasion for teaching Scripture to youngsters. Do not confine it to a religious setting on one day of the week.

I have ministered to the children of quite a number of ministers over the years. For these children religion was often a special suit they put on to go to church on Sundays. They wore it back home again, took it off, put it into the closet and did not wear it again until the next Sunday. This was the fault of the parents—because faith, to be worth anything, must be part of the daily life of the home.

I mentioned in chapter 1 that Lydia, before I married her, was mother to eight adopted girls whom she raised on her own. As a family they were short on money and often had no promise of food for the next day. One thing Lydia did was get the girls praying with her. "Children," she would say, "we've got nothing for breakfast. We'd better pray."

They all prayed and food came. Seeing God answer their prayers taught the children more about Him than a dozen lessons in Sunday school!

Never keep children out of your spiritual life. Bring them into it. If you are going on vacation, pray together about where you will go and what you will do. If a child has a problem at school, do not just supply the correct answer. Instead say, "Let's pray together about it."

When children learn to pray, they grow up believers. I can say that from experience. None of our girls has ever been without temptation. They have all had their trials and problems. But all remember times in their lives when God answered their prayers.

When Lydia and I were serving as educational missionaries in Kenya, we took our daughter Elisabeth, who was eighteen at the time, with us to a Christian conference in Mombasa. Elisabeth was very nearsighted and her eyesight was deteriorating. Every year we had to get her stronger glasses. So we said to the preacher in Mombasa, "Would you pray for Elisabeth's eyes?"

He prayed and Elisabeth took off her glasses. We did not tell her to do that!

A few days later we wondered how Elisabeth was doing. "How are your eyes?" we asked.

"Well" she replied, "he prayed, didn't he?"

Later Elisabeth's vision tested perfect and she graduated from nursing school without the use of glasses!

Our daughter Elisabeth went through the same kinds of tests that all Christians face. But there was one thing she would never doubt: *God is real!* What was her evidence? Her eyesight!

An experience of answered prayer is an anchor when people are in danger of being swept away by the tide of this world. So let them remember something that happened when you prayed with them.

A close friend of mine is a minister with four daughters. They were like Philip's daughters: While they were still children, each had a prophetic ministry (see Acts 21:8–9) and a special prayer responsibility. One prayed for finance, the second for healing, the third for problems at school and the fourth for some other need. Because those girls shared in the spiritual life of the family, they were rooted in Christ. As a result the family stayed in a close relationship, even after the girls had married.

You do not bless children by taking all the responsibility from them. On the contrary, the more you commit to them, the stronger they will grow. But do it gradually and with wisdom.

3. Communicating Both Ways

In order to teach your family about God, you need to have clear lines of communication. Many books and teachers offer instruction on how to communicate, but I want to offer you a few of my own observations.

First, the most effective communication between a father and child usually takes place in a nonreligious setting. If children associate their fathers' instruction with something stiff, formal and religious, in the end they tend to resent both the faith and the instruction.

Another principle essential in communicating with children is not merely to talk to them, but to let them talk to you. Most people who deal with wayward or delinquent children agree that nearly all these youngsters have one common complaint: *Our parents never listen to us.* Encourage children to express themselves and to explain their problems. Do not make the atmosphere too religious, and do not look shocked at some of the things they tell you!

Finally, the most important things you say to your child are often said in a casual or offhand way at a time you least expect it—gardening, mowing, on a fishing trip, cleaning out the garage, finding out why the car will not run. This is when you may be able to transmit to your son or daughter the deep principles of the Word of God. Just having a "family altar" by itself will not necessarily do it. A lot depends on how your family spends the rest of the time. Everyday situations lend themselves to real communication.

4. Saving Your Family in the Last Days

I have taught many times on the Scripture, "As it was in the days of Noah, so it will be also in the days of the Son of Man" (Luke 17:26). I always point out that the evils of the days of Noah are being played out in front of our eyes today. But one day I saw the positive message in Noah's story: "By faith Noah, being divinely warned of things not yet seen, moved with godly fear, prepared an ark for the saving of his household. . ." (Hebrews 11:7). Noah, the righteous man, heard from God about the disaster that was coming, made preparation and saved his family.

The days in which we now live are becoming more and more like the days of Noah. One particular feature of Noah's day was that "the earth [was] filled with violence" (Genesis 6:13). That is certainly true of the earth today! Crimes of violence are becoming increasingly common. Having grown up in Britain between the two world wars, I can remember when a thief breaking into a car and stealing a woman's handbag would have made the headlines. Today major crimes of violence are so common they are scarcely even reported. You may also remember more recently when it was possible to board an airplane without any security check. Not today!

The Father as Prophet

Let me relate briefly two incidents in which a father's sensitivity saved one or more members of his family from possible death.

One of my grandsons was driving the family van with his wife and three small children as passengers. Normally his wife would have sat in the passenger seat beside him, but it was arranged for some reason that she would sit in the back seat with the three small children.

As the van passed under an overpass, someone dropped a lump of concrete onto it. The windshield in front of the passenger seat was shattered and everyone inside was covered with powdered glass. But no one in the family received the slightest injury. Only at that point did the parents understand why they had been restrained from putting anyone in the front seat beside the driver. Had anyone been in that seat, the result would have been entirely different.

The second incident concerns a friend of mine, whom we will call Malcolm. He had a premonition one night that some kind of danger was threatening a member of his family.

The next morning, when his daughter was getting ready to drive to work in her mother's car, as she did each day, Malcolm told her, "This morning I feel you'd better take my car, not your mother's."

Driving in her father's car, the girl came to a patch of road on which oil had spilled. The car skidded out of control and crashed, but the girl was spared critical injury because the airbag inflated. Had she been driving her mother's car, which had no airbag, the accident would probably have been fatal.

The days in which we live call for fathers with a prophetic spirit like Noah—fathers who will be sensitive to intimations of danger facing their families and who will take protective action on their behalf.

10

The Father as King

Let's review the three main functions of a father. As priest he represents his family to God. As prophet he represents God to his family. Finally, as king, he governs his family on behalf of God.

Just what does it mean for a father to be a king?

In 1 Timothy 3:4–5 Paul discusses the qualifications for a man who wants to be a leader in the church. The most important area of all, writes Paul, is the condition of the man's home. Such a man "must manage his own family well and see that his children obey him with proper respect" (1 Timothy 3:4, NIV). He is expected to exercise authority and to have his children respectful, obedient and under his control.

The Greek word translated manage means literally "to stand out in front of" or "to stand at the head of." It contains various related ideas, including "to rule," "to protect" and "to control." Essentially the word means that the father stands at the head of the home. He puts himself between his family and all the pressures and dangers of life. He also goes in front of them and sets an example of godly living.

Successful leadership at home, Paul goes on to say, is essential for leadership in the church. "If a man does not know how to rule his own house," he asks, "how will he take care of the church of God?" (verse 5). If a man cannot achieve successful leadership at home, in other words, he cannot expect to succeed as a leader in God's church.

At one time I enjoyed a brief acquaintance with Lewi Pethrus of Sweden, who pastored the largest Pentecostal church in Europe through the period of World War II. He was a man who took very seriously the biblical requirements for being a pastor.

At one point he came before his congregation and told them he was resigning as their pastor.

"Scripture says that I must have my children in subjection," he explained, "but my sons are not walking with the Lord. So I must resign."

"Don't do that!" the people responded. "We'll pray for your sons that they may be saved."

The people prayed, the sons were saved and Pastor Pethrus did not resign.

Unfortunately many men in the ministry today do not take the requirements of Scripture so seriously.

There is a logical reason that success as a father should be a requirement for holding the office of pastor. The home is really the church in miniature.

In a New Testament church there were three main elements:

1. The pastor or shepherd (usually plural—also called "elders")
2. Deacons or helpers
3. The congregation or flock

These correspond to the three main elements in the home:

1. The father, who has the responsibility of pastor or shepherd

2. The wife, who was created to help her husband just as a deacon helps the pastor
3. The children, who are the congregation or flock

God has built into the family, then, all the basics that make up a proper New Testament church. God says to the father of the family, in effect: "Cause your little church to succeed—the one I have committed to you in your own home—and then you will qualify for promotion in the Church of God."

Walking in Abraham's Steps

We turn now to Abraham as a picture of a father who accepted and fulfilled his responsibility to rule or be king of his family.

Have you ever wondered why God chose Abraham out of the hundreds of thousands of men on earth at that day? Why was Abraham privileged to head a new race that would bring salvation to all humanity?

First look at the meaning of Abraham's name. Originally it was *Abram,* which means "exalted father." Then, when God made His second and eternal covenant with this man, He changed his name to Abraham, which means "father of a multitude." You can see in both forms that the first fact about his name is that he was a father. That is tremendously significant. God chose Abraham *as a father.*

Next let us look at something important that God said about Abraham:

Shall I hide from Abraham that thing which I do; seeing that Abraham shall surely become a great and mighty nation, and all the nations of the earth shall be blessed in him? For I know him, that he will command his children and his household after him, and they shall keep the way of the Lord, to do justice and judgment; that the Lord may bring upon Abraham that which he hath spoken of him.

Genesis 18:17–19, KJV

The New International Version says, "I have chosen him, so that he will direct his children..." (verse 19). The word here translated "direct" is the standard Hebrew word for "command." It is used regularly with that sense in all the ordinances of Moses. Whichever translation we follow, the fact of the matter is, Abraham was eligible for God's choice because God could rely on him to *command* his children and household.

The word *command* is a strong word, almost a military word. Some wives and mothers may say, "Are you talking about the man being a dictator?" No. There are some situations, however, in which the man is responsible to say, "In order to please God and have His blessing, this is the way we're going to do things in our home. We are not going to do this, but we are going to do that."

A father has the right, I believe, to determine some of the basic rules of the household: what time they will eat together, what time the younger children must come in, the kind of entertainment the children are permitted, the use of the television and so on. This is not merely the father's privilege; it is his duty.

A father should not make decisions such as these, of course, without first consulting his wife and making sure she is in agreement. Nevertheless the final responsibility for order in the house rests with the father. He is the one who must answer to God for his family.

In Romans 4:11–12 we are told that Abraham is a father to all those who *walk in his steps*. That means I cannot just say, "I'm born again, and therefore Abraham is my father." I have to walk the way Abraham walked. In no area is this more important than in the family.

Order in the Heavenly Family

For the perfect pattern of authority in the family, we should look to the divine family in heaven. How does authority work in relationship between God the Father and God the Son?

The way Jesus spoke about His relationship to His Father challenges some contemporary theories about raising children:

> "The reason my Father loves me is that I lay down my life—only to take it up again. No one takes it from me, but I lay it down of my own accord. I have authority to lay it down and authority to take it up again. This command I received from my Father."
>
> John 10:17–18, NIV

This makes it clear that God the Father gave commands and Jesus the Son carried them out.

Again, in John 12:49–50, Jesus said:

> "I have not spoken on My own authority; but the Father who sent Me gave Me a command, what I should say and what I should speak. And I know that His command is everlasting life. Therefore, whatever I speak, just as the Father has told Me, so I speak."

In all His teaching, therefore, Jesus was obeying a *command* that He had received from God His Father.

Further on, in John 14:31, as Jesus prepared to leave the Upper Room and face the encounter that led to His trial and execution, He said:

> "The world must learn that I love the Father and that I do exactly what my Father has commanded me. Come now; let us leave."
>
> NIV

So Jesus went to the cross in obedience to His Father's command. That was the ultimate test of obedience!

In Hebrews 5:8 the writer sums this all up in one simple sentence: "Though He [Jesus] was a Son, yet He *learned obedience* by the things which He suffered."

Here is the pattern, then, of two divine Persons—the Father and the Son. The Father gave the commands and the Son learned obedience by obeying the commands. His obedience cost Him His life. There is no biblical pattern for sloppiness or disobedience or carelessness. God is a precise God. He tells us exactly what He wants us to do and He expects us to do it.

This pattern should be reproduced in the human family. We on earth have no liberty to improve on the pattern set for us in heaven.

Discipline in the Home

We just saw from Hebrews 5:8 that Jesus had to *learn* obedience. This indicates that obedience needs to be *taught*. Teaching obedience is what we call *discipline*. If even Jesus needed to submit to discipline, how much more do we and our precious—but imperfect—children!

If you want to raise your children successfully, you must combine love with discipline. The way to produce unhappy, frustrated children, on the other hand, is to spoil them—to give them all they ask for, to do everything they want, to succumb to every demand. Children raised in this way will, when they grow up, expect life to treat them the same way their parents did. But life does not play the game that way! Life is pretty tough—and getting tougher. I have observed the lives of people whose parents treated them with unscriptural indulgence and I would say that, in varying degrees, they have all had difficult lives.

To spoil your children is not kindness. Often, in fact, it is the expression of *laziness*. It takes much less effort to spoil your children than to discipline them.

The most unhappy children are the ones with no discipline in their lives. They are also the most insecure—because a child needs to have boundaries that give him security.

I remember when my African daughter, Jesika, was about sixteen years old and going through some of the problems teenagers go through. Although she was a sincere Christian, she wanted to do something at one point that was neither wise nor right.

"Can I do it?" she asked. "Will you let me?"

"No, I won't," I said, "because it will be bad for you."

I anticipated that Jesika would be upset. But I saw in her eyes relief that I had set a boundary. She did not have the strength in herself to make her own boundary, but she was grateful to me for setting one for her.

It is unfair to turn children loose—especially in the world as it is today—with no boundaries. Those boundaries should be simple and practical, and usually they should be explained to children:

"Why don't we watch such-and-such a program on television?"

"Because it sets you a bad example and encourages you to do things that are harmful to you."

There may be a few situations, on the other hand, in which the answer to "Why?" is simply "Because Daddy [or Mother] says." Giving a reason for some regulations may be too complicated for a small child to comprehend. After all, our Father God sometimes makes rules for His people without giving us all His reasons. I doubt, for instance, whether most Israelis understood all the reasons for God's dietary regulations in Leviticus 11. Yet God still expected them to obey!

While our children were growing up, one portion of Scripture Lydia and I gave them to memorize was 1 Samuel 15:22: "To obey is better than sacrifice, and to hearken than the fat of rams" (KJV). Years later I was amused to discover some of them teaching the same Scripture to their children!

In the next chapter I will continue our study of fatherhood by contrasting two fathers described in the book of Genesis.

11

A Picture of Two Fathers

There was one man who played a significant role in the life of Abraham. He was Abraham's nephew, Lot. The two men had been through much together. Undoubtedly Lot had observed God's dealings with Abraham and had come into his own personal relationship with the Lord. The time came, however, when the two men had to separate, for "the land could not support them while they stayed together, for their possessions were so great that they were not able to stay together" (Genesis 13:6, NIV).

Abraham allowed Lot to choose where he would go. The act of separation brought out a decisive difference in the two men—a difference of *vision*.

Abraham's vision stretched beyond the things of time— out of this world into an eternal future:

> He was looking forward to the city with foundations, whose architect and builder is God.
>
> Hebrews 11:10, NIV

Abraham made his choices in life with his eyes fixed on an eternal destination.

Lot, on the other hand, saw no further than his present surroundings:

> Lot looked up and saw that the whole plain of the Jordan was well watered, like the garden of the LORD, like the land of Egypt, toward Zoar. (This was before the LORD destroyed Sodom and Gomorrah.) So Lot chose for himself the whole plain of the Jordan and set out toward the east. The two men parted company: Abram lived in the land of Canaan, while Lot lived among the cities of the plain and pitched his tents near Sodom.
>
> Genesis 13:10–12, NIV

In the next verse the biblical writer adds, almost parenthetically:

> But the men of Sodom were exceedingly wicked and sinful against the LORD.
>
> verse 13

Lot's vision determined the course he took. He was irresistibly drawn toward the wealth and fertility of Sodom and was blind to the extreme sinfulness and perversion of Sodom's inhabitants.

Some years later God sent two angels to Sodom to proclaim His impending judgment on the city. By this time Lot no longer simply had his face turned toward Sodom. He was right inside the city, actually "sitting in the gate" (Genesis 19:1). This would indicate that Lot held a position of authority in the community. Even though he had not followed the sinful practices of the people, he had made himself one with them.

The angels warned Lot urgently to gather all the members of his family—"son-in-law, your sons, your daughters, and whomever you have in the city" (Genesis 19:12)—and to escape with them before the city was destroyed.

So Lot went out and spoke to his sons-in-law, who had married his daughters, and said, "Get up, get out of this place; for the LORD will destroy this city!" But to his sons-in-law he seemed to be joking.

verse 14

Because the idea of God's judgment seemed ridiculous to his sons-in-law, eventually Lot managed to take with him only his wife and two unmarried daughters. Even then, outside the city, his wife turned back for one last, regretful look at all she was leaving behind and she was turned into a pillar of salt.

Later I picture Lot—from the safety of the mountains to which he had fled—looking down on the smoldering ruins that had once been Sodom, and on the pillar of salt that had once been his wife. "I led my whole family into that place," he might have said, "but the only ones who followed me out were these two daughters of mine." (We might note that even they became involved in an incestuous relationship with their father.)

Was Lot crushed by an overwhelming sense of guilt as he realized how he had failed to fulfill his responsibility to his family? Scripture gives us no answer to this question. But let me suggest to you, if you are a father, that for a few moments you put yourself in Lot's place. Can you imagine yourself thinking, *If only I had made different choices! If only I had stayed closer to Abraham!*

Now ask yourself several pivotal questions:

What kind of example have I been setting for my family? Am I giving them eternal purposes and eternal standards to live by? Or am I compromising my standards and commitments for the sake of material prosperity and worldly success?

Each of these two men, Abraham and Lot, had a vision. Abraham's vision focused on a glorious, eternal city that God has prepared for His servants who follow Him wholly. Lot's vision focused on the material prosperity of an earthly city and blinded him to the sinfulness of its inhabitants. Each man's vision determined not only the course in life that he himself followed, but also the destiny of his family.

Many centuries later this principle still holds true: *A father imparts to his family the vision that directs his own life.* Every father needs to ask himself, therefore, the following questions:

What vision am I imparting to my family? Am I inculcating eternal values that will direct them into lives of service for Jesus Christ? Or am I concerned primarily with worldly success—a career, material comfort, financial independence, status in the community?

I once heard a talk by the president of a well-known evangelical college. The majority of the parents who send their children to that college are professing Christians. But the president had this to say:

"I make it a point at some point to ask each of my students, 'When your parents sent you to this college, what did they tell you was the most important thing in your future? Was it to become a faithful servant of Jesus Christ?'

"Up to this point," the president continued, "none of my students has ever answered yes."

If your son or daughter were to be enrolled in that college, how would he or she answer?

12

When Fathers Fail

In the preceding chapters I have outlined the three God-given responsibilities every father has toward his family: as *priest*, to intercede for them; as *prophet*, to represent God to them; as *king*, to rule them according to God's standards of righteousness.

In the last chapter we saw that Lot's failure to fulfill his duties as a father brought disaster on his whole family. By contrast we observed that God chose Abraham because He could rely on him to be faithful in his duties as a father, on which basis God promised him that he would become the head of a great and mighty nation.

This suggests an important question: If faithful fatherhood produces a blessed and prosperous nation, what will happen to a nation whose fathers fail in their primary obligations? In Deuteronomy 28 Moses provides a vivid picture of what we may expect.

This chapter of Deuteronomy falls naturally into two sections. In the first fourteen verses Moses lists all the blessings that will come on God's people if they obey Him. In the remaining 54 verses Moses lists the curses that will come on them if they disobey Him.

One verse in this latter section describes one of the curses that will come on a nation whose fathers fail in their duties toward their families:

> Thou shalt beget sons and daughters, but thou shalt not enjoy them; for they shall go into captivity.
>
> Deuteronomy 28:41, KJV

The Hebrew words here indicate that Moses is speaking to men. The word *beget* refers primarily to the father's part in procreating children. So this verse is addressed primarily (but not exclusively) to fathers.

I realized with a shock one day that not enjoying our children is a curse. I began to ask myself, *How many parents today really enjoy their children?* Not many, I concluded. What is the reason? I believe it is a curse for disobedience. God made children the greatest blessing He could give to men and women. When fathers and mothers—but especially fathers—do not walk in the way of the Lord, then their sons and daughters are no longer a blessing but a curse.

The New American Standard Bible translates Deuteronomy 28:41 more literally: "You shall have [beget] sons and daughters, but they will not be yours...." This, too, is being fulfilled today. In countless broken families the children no longer belong to their parents. Parents and children are estranged from one another. This again is the outworking of a curse.

Moses warned that the children would "go into captivity" (verse 41). Since 1960 we in the Western world have seen millions of children go into different kinds of satanic captivity—to drugs, illicit sex, the occult and various types of cults. Those who are enslaved by these things are in captivity just as surely as if an invading alien army had marched into the country and carried them off as prisoners.

Why have millions of children gone into captivity? We see the answer in Deuteronomy 28: persistent rejection of God's righteous requirements, especially in home and family.

As I pointed out in chapter 9, Hebrew verbs and pronouns use different forms for masculine and feminine. In Deuteronomy 28 all the verbs appear in the masculine form. God places the primary responsibility, in other words, on men. This does not mean women do not carry their share of responsibility. Certainly they do. But it is the failure of male leadership that opens the way for all the other evils that follow.

And it is the pattern of evils in the Garden of Eden that has been repeated countless times in subsequent human history. Adam was delinquent in his responsibility to guard the Garden, which opened the way for Satan to tempt and seduce Eve. The delinquency of men has likewise opened the way to the flood of evil that has now engulfed Western civilization.

In Malachi 2:7 the prophet points out one main responsibility that the father, as priest, has toward his family:

> "The lips of a priest should keep knowledge, and people should seek the law from his mouth; for he is the messenger of the Lord of hosts."

The priest is responsible to know the law of the Lord and to interpret it to the Lord's people. This also applies to a father as priest. His children and family should seek the word of the Lord from his mouth.

What happens if priests fail in their function? God declares:

> "My people are destroyed for lack of knowledge. Because you have rejected knowledge, I also will reject you

from being priest for Me; because you have forgotten the law of your God, I also will forget your children."

Hosea 4:6

What a powerful word! God is telling the Israelites, "I expected you to be priests, but you rejected the knowledge you needed." This was not secular knowledge they rejected, but knowledge of the way and word of the Lord. As a result God no longer accepts them as priests—and even vows to forget their children.

As priest of his family, each father has the privilege to do what Job did—to bear up his children continuously before God in prayer. This keeps them under the continuing oversight and protection of the Almighty. But when a father fails to fulfill his intercessory ministry as priest, God says, "I will forget your children." The NIV renders this, "I also will *ignore* your children" (emphasis added). That is, "Your children will no longer be under My special, watchful care."

This solemn warning of God has become vivid to me these days. Sometimes, watching the multitudes of young people thronging the streets in a city, I ask myself, *How many of these are forgotten by God—ignored by God—because they have no fathers to intercede for them?*

This terrible situation calls for an army of committed intercessors who will stand in the gap on behalf of such families. But the intercessory prayer of a father on behalf of his family is unique. No one else can fully take that father's place. His unique privileges carry with them unique responsibilities.

Malachi's Diagnosis

Chronologically Malachi is the last book of the Old Testament. Furthermore the last word in this last book is *curse*.

101

If God had no more to say to humanity after the Old Testament, His last word would have been a curse. Thank God for the New Testament, which shows the way out of the curse!

This is what God says in the last two verses of the Old Testament:

> "Behold, I will send you Elijah the prophet before the coming of the great and dreadful day of the LORD. And he will turn the hearts of the fathers to the children, and the hearts of the children to their fathers, lest I come and strike the earth with a curse."

Malachi 4:5–6

Well over two thousand years ago, God revealed to Malachi through prophetic foresight the greatest and most urgent problem of our day: delinquent fathers and unparented children.

Economists and social legislators offer us all sorts of diagnoses and solutions. The real root of the problem, however, is in the family. Parents have reneged on their responsibilities to their children. Often both parents are guilty, but the primary responsibility rests on the fathers.

We must acknowledge that the women's liberation movement has in some ways backfired. Apart from making headway toward equal pay for equal work, women have been liberated from their commitment to honor and obey their husbands. The husband, in turn, has been liberated from his commitment to be faithful to one woman. So the man gets tired of his wife and walks out. After that he has no more obligations, while the woman is left struggling to raise one or more children on her own. In most cases she is worse off than she was before.

I have deep concern in my heart for single mothers. In many cases, it seems to me, the contemporary Church is not doing what she should for single mothers and their children.

In James 1:27 the Bible offers us a definition of what God considers true religion:

> Pure and undefiled religion before God and the Father is this: to visit orphans and widows in their trouble, and to keep oneself unspotted from the world.

Sometimes I ask myself what would happen if every Christian family who takes the Bible seriously were to accept responsibility for just one child who is in effect, if not in name, an orphan? That would include every child without proper parental care or provision. Certainly it would require the sacrifice of some degree of comfort and convenience. Perhaps there would also be some financial sacrifice. But if this were done in a spirit of Christian love, it would relieve a measure of suffering so vast that most of us try not to think about it.

Unfortunately our refusal to think about it does not make the need any less real or any less urgent. Almost against my will I am reminded of the words of Jesus in Matthew 25 spoken to the "goat" nations: "Inasmuch as you did not do it. . ." (verse 45). As Christians of the Western world, we shall be judged not so much for what we have done as for what we have not done.

Malachi's message was addressed to people extremely zealous in their religious practices, yet who complained that the Lord did not answer their prayers as they expected. In response the Lord pointed out their failures as husbands and fathers:

> You flood the Lord's altar with tears. You weep and wail because he no longer pays attention to your offerings or accepts them with pleasure from your hands. You ask, "Why?" It is because the Lord is acting as the witness between you and the wife of your youth, because you have broken faith with her, though she is your partner, the wife of your marriage covenant.
>
> Malachi 2:13–14, NIV

God looked behind all their external religiosity and saw broken marriage vows and husbands abusing wives. In contemporary speech Malachi's message might be summarized like this: "Nothing you do in church makes up for what you don't do at home."

God went on to explain one main purpose of a monogamous marriage as He originally ordained it: "Has not the LORD made them one? In flesh and spirit they are his. And why one? *Because he was seeking godly offspring*" (Malachi 2:15, NIV, emphasis added).

When husband and wife live together in harmony according to the principles of Scripture, they are qualified to raise righteous, God-fearing children. And when a marriage breaks up, it is the children who suffer the most.

God continued with a warning to all husbands: "So guard yourself in your spirit, and do not break faith with the wife of your youth" (Malachi 2:15, NIV). He followed this with an uncompromising statement of His attitude toward divorce: "For the LORD God of Israel says that He hates divorce" (verse 16).

How Will You Respond?

In every government office in Britain, where marriages may be registered, this definition of marriage is prominently displayed: "According to the law of this country, marriage is the union of one man with one woman for life, to the exclusion of all others." Over the period that the British people have departed further and further from this standard, their country has undergone a steady decline in almost every area of national life. Few people today bother any longer to put the "Great" in front of "Britain"!

God's Word confronts not only Britain but our whole Western civilization with just two alternatives: We may either restore family relationships and survive, or we may allow family relationships to continue to deteriorate and go the way they have been going in the last decades. If we do, we will perish under God's curse.

The final outcome of this crisis will be decided by the response of the fathers. They are the ones whom God holds primarily responsible. In God's message through Malachi, He requires first that the hearts of the fathers turn to the children. Only after that will the hearts of the children turn to the fathers.

Those of us who belong to older generations can complain about Generation X or Generation Next or whatever we may call them. We can point out all their faults and failings. But the crisis did not begin with them. It is the older generations who are to blame. It is our generations who have betrayed them, who have failed to present the truth to them, who have failed to teach them godly discipline. Now God is judging us through our children.

There are voices crying out that the Church today needs to become socially relevant. In no area in society does the Church have a greater opportunity to become socially relevant than in the area of family life. In so doing we shall be responding to the most urgent crisis of our time.

The Church today needs to present a clear message depicting the Christian family as God intended it to be— a message that defines the roles of husbands, wives and children. But it must be a message faithful to the great, unchanging principles established in Scripture from Genesis onward. There must be no compromise with the humanistic forces that have infiltrated the Church in the last three or four generations.

In the Sermon on the Mount Jesus warned His disciples that their commitment to follow Him would focus people's attention on them: "You are the light of the world. A city that is set on a hill cannot be hidden" (Matthew 5:14).

Then He continued, "Let your light so shine before men, that they may see your good works and glorify your Father in heaven" (verse 16).

Jesus was telling His disciples not only that He expected them to be a source of light in a darkened world. He was also telling them just how their light was to shine: through their good works made visible to all.

In the preceding chapters we have seen that God intends the Christian family to be a source of light to a darkened world, in two main ways. First, husbands and wives, by the way they relate to each other, are to depict the relationship between Christ and His Church. Second, fathers are to build families that depict the love of God as a Father to His believing people. The Bible also reveals one primary good work God expects from His people: to care for orphans and widows. This requirement is stated in many places in the Old Testament and is reemphasized in the New.

All Summed Up in One Word

God's requirements may all be summed up in a single word of fathomless meaning: *love*. This love is manifested in three main dimensions:

1. The intimate love between a husband and his wife
2. The protective love of parents for their children
3. The reaching out love of believers toward those who have no one else to love them—the orphans and widows

If the contemporary Western Church is a "city . . . set on a hill [that] cannot be hidden," we need to ask: *How does the Church appear to the non-Christian world all around?* In particular, *does the world see the Church fulfilling her responsibility to demonstrate the divine love between Christ and His Church and the Fatherly love of God for His family?* We also need to ask: *Does the world see the Church setting an example by the way she cares for orphans and widows?*

These are questions that demand an answer. We cannot shrug our shoulders and ignore them. Probably each person has to give his or her own answer.

My answer is based on long and wide experience to many nations. I have held citizenship in both Britain and the U.S.A. I have ministered in more than fifty nations, including every nation in Europe except Finland and Bulgaria, and in all the main English-speaking nations. My frank, personal conclusion is that the contemporary Church is *delinquent.* Thank God, there are some wonderful exceptions, but for the most part the Church has not been demonstrating the love of God, either in her basic family relationships or in her care for orphans and widows.

Various Christian organizations are seeking to confront the contemporary failure of male leadership and the resultant breakdown of the family—organizations like Focus on the Family, under the leadership of Dr. James Dobson, and, more recently, Promise Keepers. We need to ask ourselves why these and other parachurch groups have multiplied in the latter half of the twentieth century. The answer in most cases is that they are seeking to carry out tasks that Jesus committed originally to the Church.

While we may admire and support these parachurch groups, I do not believe this shift of responsibility is ultimately acceptable to Jesus, the Head of the Church. He still requires the Church to acknowledge her responsibilities and He waits for her to fulfill them. Obviously this will require a major revolution in the Church as she is functioning presently. Failing that, I believe Jesus will set aside the contemporary Church and raise up in her place a Church that is fit to become His bride.

There is much talk and prayer these days focusing on the theme of revival. One mark of true revival will be that the Church as a whole acknowledges and accepts her responsibility to carry out the tasks that are often left at present to parachurch organizations.

One thing is sure: Jesus is not coming back for a parachurch. He is coming for a bride who "has made herself ready" and who is clothed in "fine linen, clean and bright . . . the righteous acts of His saints" (Revelation 19:7–8). Professing Christians who do not carry out the "righteous acts" assigned to them will have no fabric for their bridal attire and will therefore not be eligible to attend the wedding.

As I survey the contemporary Church in the Western world, I keep recalling the words with which Jesus dispatched the "goat" nations to a lost eternity: "Inasmuch as you did not do it. . . ." We need to remember that they were cursed not for what they did but for what they did not do.

13

Perhaps You Have Failed?

Now that you have read this far, it is time to pause and reflect. Possibly you have come face to face for the first time with a biblical picture of what God expects a father to be and to do—and you are shocked!

Do not react too quickly. Take time to think—and to pray—about this issue. Ask God to make the picture clearer to you. Perhaps it will help you to read through the preceding five chapters once again.

And remember Paul's definition of sin in Romans 3:23: "All have sinned and fall short of the glory of God." Sin is not necessarily doing something wicked. In essence it is acting and living in such a way that God does not receive from our lives the glory that is due Him. Remember, too, that men are often guilty of sins of *omission*—sinning by what we fail to do.

There are moments in our lives when we need to judge ourselves. If we do this, we can claim the mercy promised in 1 Corinthians 11:31: "If we would judge ourselves, we would not be judged."

Consider the three primary ministries of a father to his family: priest, prophet and king. Check your performance in each of these three areas, and ask yourself some relevant questions:

> As priest of my family, am I faithful in regular, daily intercession for them? How often do I thank God for them?
>
> As prophet, how well have I represented God to my family? Have I given them a picture of the loving Father in heaven? Or must I acknowledge that the picture I have given them of our Father God is actually an unattractive caricature?
>
> As king, have I ruled my children with a discipline that combines love and firmness and that prepares them to take their place in society as responsible citizens? Have I set boundaries for my children that protect them from the evil forces at work in the world today?

What is your response to these questions? Do you recognize that you have indeed "sinned and [fallen] short of the glory of God"? That is no reason to be discouraged or to give up. God convicts us of our sins not in order to condemn us but to direct us to the remedy He has provided for us through the sacrifice of Jesus Christ on the cross.

Two Simple Steps

God's simple requirement is stated in 1 John 1:9: "If we confess our sins, He is faithful and just to forgive us our sins and to cleanse us from all unrighteousness." When we sincerely acknowledge and confess our sins to God, He not only forgives us but He also cleanses us from all sense of guilt and failure and restores to us pure consciences.

To complete the cure, there is one further step we need to take. Our personal relationships are like the two beams that form the cross: one vertical, the other horizontal. The vertical beam represents our relationship with God; the horizontal beam represents our relationship with our fellow human beings. In putting things right, the first step is *to take care of our relationship with God by confessing our sins to Him and receiving His forgiveness*. The second step is *to put things right with our fellow men by confessing our sins to them*.

This requirement is stated in James 5:16: "Confess your sins to each other and pray for each other so that you may be healed. The prayer of a righteous man is powerful and effective" (NIV). Far too little is said in the contemporary Church about the need to confess our sins to one another. Consequently the atmosphere in many Christian groups is poisoned by sins that have not been confessed and by attitudes of resentment and bitterness that have never been resolved. This inhibits the working of the Holy Spirit.

John Wesley recorded in his journal that one of the most successful of the early Methodist societies grew out of a group of about ten people who agreed to meet weekly and confess their sins to one another.

In 1 John 1:7 the apostle states the primary requirement for continuing spiritual purity: "If we walk in the light as He is in the light, we have fellowship with one another, and the blood of Jesus Christ His Son cleanses us from all sin." "Walking in the light" entails being honest and open with each other. All the verbs in this verse are in the continuing present tense: "If we *continually* walk . . . *continually* have fellowship . . . the blood *continually* cleanses. . . ." In other words John is depicting a continuing lifestyle.

This requirement applies to all Christians living in fellowship, but first and foremost to the Christian family. This places a special responsibility in turn on the father in each family.

A Father Who Confessed

Let us suppose you have taken the first step and confessed your sins to God. Now you need to take the next step and confess your sins to the members of your family—first to your wife and then to your children.

Quite probably you are already aware of some of the sins you need to confess, but up till now you have been sweeping them under the rug. Let me tell you frankly, there is no rug ever made that will cover those sins!

As I was working on this chapter in my manuscript, I received an unexpected letter from a Christian couple I have known for several years. We will call them David and Rosemary.

Some months previously David had decided to go on a special kind of fast—to abstain not primarily from food but from other distractions that crowd in on us and make us insensitive to the voice of the Spirit. His list included television, the movies and various kinds of recorded music.

In her letter Rosemary shared some of what the fast had brought out in their lives. I quote below excerpts from what she said:

> It seems right now that what God began earlier—and is continuing to do—is to show us how much dirt and muck has been in our hearts. I'm sure that if He chose to show me *all* my sin at once, I would die on the spot. But in His gentle, merciful way He shows us, little by little, that which is displeasing to Him. And there has been *so* much. I feel as if I have been confessing sin for months on end . . . and David, too.
>
> At the very beginning of the fast, the Lord showed David very clearly that the entire fast would be for noth-

ing if he had unconfessed sin in his life. So he confessed it all out to the Lord and repented. Then the Lord said, "Now tell your wife!" And with much pain, humility and sorrow, he spilled out hidden sins that I never knew of or suspected. God clearly brought us to this place and sustained us beautifully with Scripture and reassurances.

David's confession was a real wake-up call to both of us, and to our close friends with whom we shared some of this. God used this situation to show us how easily the mindset of the world colors our perspective, how easily we let sin slip in till it has taken over, and how much we rely on ourselves instead of on God. Time and again God has shown us how we haven't guarded our hearts. God has shown both of us things that had become idols. David got rid of almost all his extensive music collection. This was something I could never have persuaded him to do on my own, so I *knew* it was God.

In three words I would describe what has taken place in us: pain, purification, revival. I now understand what revival really is about. It doesn't happen in a building or to a mass of people at once, but in a heart yielded to His glorious love and responding to His wooing and correction. I have been amazed, and thankful, at how gentle God is in dealing with me. His correction is merciful and restorative.

There are some wonderful things that have come since the beginnings of this. Some months ago David asked a group of men to share breakfast every other Monday morning. The goal was to pray for each other and just share their lives. Out of this group of men, since David told them what has happened in us, almost every one of them has gone to his wife and confessed some aspect of hidden sin. God is doing this purifying in all of them!

Now the wives of this group have started meeting to pray for our husbands. It has been the most beautiful, natural outpouring of the Holy Spirit I have ever experienced. By *natural* I mean this: None of us goes to the same church. This outpouring isn't happening in a building; it is simply the Body of Christ ministering to each other. It has been awesome! And because we don't all go to the same church, we are sharing what is happening with those in our churches, and it seems to be spreading!

What is taking place in this family needs to happen in millions of families where there is unconfessed sin in the life of the father. Many Christians are conscious of sins they have not confessed, but they adopt the attitude that "if I ignore this thing long enough, it will go away." That is a deception! There is only one way to deal effectively with sin—heartfelt repentance followed by confession: "He who covers his sins will not prosper, but whoever confesses and forsakes them will have mercy" (Proverbs 28:13).

This brings out the real barrier in dealing with sin: *pride. If I confess these sins*, we say to ourselves, *I'll be humiliated.* No, that is another deception! If you confess your sins, you will be *humbled.* If you refuse to confess them, ultimately you will be *humiliated.*

God never offers to make us humble. Invariably His message is: "Humble yourself" (see, for example, 1 Peter 5:6). That is something only you can do. No one else can make you humble—not even God! But if you refuse to humble yourself, sooner or later the time will come when you will be humiliated.

You are faced with the choice: Either humble yourself and trust God for His mercy and grace, or refuse to humble yourself and, in due course, be humiliated by circumstances outside your control.

To Whom to Confess

You may ask: To whom do I need to make my confession? Someone has given the following answer: *The confession must be as wide as the transgression.* Make your confession, then, to all who have been harmed by your sin.

All sin, first and foremost, is against God. Even though King David harmed two people by his sin—Bathsheba, whom he had seduced into committing adultery, and Uriah, her husband, whose murder he had plotted—he said to God, "Against You, You only, have I sinned, and done this evil in Your sight" (Psalm 51:4). In the searching light of the Holy Spirit, David realized that his sin was, in the first instance, an affront against a holy and awesome God.

Remember, when making your confession to God, that you are not telling Him anything about yourself that He does not already know. The purpose of confession is not to inform Him, but to bring sin out into the light, where it can be dealt with. God does not forgive sin in the dark. If we desire His forgiveness, we must expose our sin to the awesome light of His countenance.

If you are still hesitant about making your confession, let me remind you of God's simple requirement: "If we confess our sins, He is faithful and just to forgive us our sins and to cleanse us from all unrighteousness" (1 John 1:9). This word of encouragement is also a word of warning. If you will make your confession, God has committed Himself to forgive you. But He has never committed Himself to forgive sins that we are not willing to confess.

Notice, too, that when God forgives, He cleanses us from all unrighteousness connected with our sin. If you have been forgiven, you have also been cleansed from unrighteousness. If your heart has not been cleansed, this probably indicates that you have not yet been forgiven. Perhaps you have not truly repented.

In most cases the sins we confess affect other people. In such cases we are obligated, whenever possible, to make our confession to any or all the people who have been affected by our sin.

If the father of a family sins, his sin probably affects his whole family, in one way or another. The first person to whom he should normally make confession is his wife. If his children are still young and immature, he must be careful not to speak about his sin in a way that would wound their tender consciences.

Before making his confession, the father should ask God earnestly to go ahead of him and prepare the hearts of his family. He should also ask God to guide him in the time and way in which he makes his confession.

If you are sincere and open to the Holy Spirit, He will show you the specific sins you need to confess. Some sins that commonly manifest themselves in fathers are impatience, irritability and uncontrolled anger. Fathers, like all men, are also frequently tempted into some form of sexual impurity, either in act or in imagination. One sin that enslaves multitudes of men today is pornography.

The Bible never speaks of a "small" sin. In 1 John 5:17 the apostle reminds us that "all unrighteousness is sin." There is no middle ground between righteousness and sin. Anything that is not righteous is sinful.

On the other hand, the Bible does categorize some sins as "great." Joseph, for instance, when tempted to commit adultery with the wife of Potiphar, exclaimed, "How . . . can I do this *great* wickedness, and sin against God?" (Genesis 39:9, emphasis added). Like David, Joseph recognized that he would be sinning first and foremost against God.

Out of the Twilight Zone

Multitudes of Christians today are living in what I call a "spiritual twilight zone." They are not walking in the clear sunlight of God's favor on a life of unreserved obedience to God, nor are they walking in the nighttime darkness of open sin.

But the Gospel leaves no room for spiritual neutrality. If you purpose to be the kind of father God is looking for, you must be willing to open up your whole heart and life to Him. As you allow Him to expose all sin and to do His purging work in you, you will move out of the twilight zone and into the clear sunlight of God's favor. There you will begin to understand all that is involved in being a father.

14

But You Can Succeed!

After reading the previous chapters, you have come face to face with areas of failure in your life. You have recognized that you have not been the kind of father God is looking for—and that your family desperately needs.

It is time for you now to make a decision. Turn your back on your failures and commit yourself to God for the ministry of a father. If you are ready to do this, here are four steps you need to take.

1. Take Your Place as Head of Your Family

This requires a decision and a commitment. You may pray something like this: "Lord, I recognize that You hold me responsible to be the head of my family. By a decision of my will, I now accept my place and the responsibility that goes with it. I commit myself to You for this task."

But You Can Succeed!

Once you have made this commitment, God will begin to endue you with the authority a father needs to be the head of his family. This is the outworking of a principle that runs all through Scripture: God never gives responsibility without authority, and He never gives authority without responsibility.

At one point in the ministry of Jesus, a Roman centurion sent messengers to ask Him to come and heal his servant, who was at death's door. In response Jesus set out with the messengers for the centurion's house. But before He got there, the centurion sent friends to Him to say,

> "Lord, do not trouble Yourself, for I am not worthy that You should enter under my roof. Therefore I did not even think myself worthy to come to You. But say the word, and my servant will be healed. For I also am a man placed under authority, having soldiers under me. And I say to one, 'Go,' and he goes; and to another, 'Come,' and he comes; and to my servant, 'Do this,' and he does it."
>
> Luke 7:6–8

This Roman centurion recognized that Jesus' authority in the spiritual realm was analogous to his own in the military realm. He summed up in one brief phrase the essential requirement for having authority in any realm: to be *under authority*. Authority is always transmitted downward from a higher source.

At the close of Jesus' earthly ministry, He told His disciples, "All authority has been given to Me in heaven and on earth" (Matthew 28:18). All true authority throughout the universe, therefore, descends from God the Father through Jesus Christ the Son.

In 1 Corinthians 11:3 Paul describes how this chain of authority descends into every family on earth: "I want you to know that the head of every man is Christ, the head of woman is man, and the head of Christ is God." This may be represented as follows:

119

Fathers

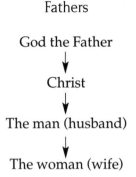

God the Father
↓
Christ
↓
The man (husband)
↓
The woman (wife)

Your authority as a husband and father, therefore, depends on your being in submission to Jesus. If you are truly submitted to Him as your Head, all the authority of heaven will flow down through you into your family, and you will function effectively as its head. If you are not in subjection to Jesus, on the other hand, you may put forth a great deal of fleshly effort—you may shout and stamp your feet; you may get angry and even violent—but you will still lack one thing: the genuine, God-given authority that alone can make you an effective head to your family.

2. Trust God for the Grace You Need

Being a father is a calling of God just as sacred as being an evangelist or a pastor. If God had called you to either of those ministries, you would not depend solely on your own ability. You would seek Him for the special grace you would need to succeed. In the same way, therefore, trust God for the grace you need to be a successful father.

Here are some words from Hebrews 4:16 to encourage you:

> Let us therefore come boldly to the throne of grace, that we may obtain mercy and find grace to help in time of need.

Recognize that through Jesus you have direct access to the throne of God, who rules the entire universe and has every situation and person under His control. Take note, too, that it is a throne of *grace*, from which is dispensed the free, unmerited favor of God to all who come through the sacrifice of Jesus on the cross. You are invited to come boldly, not hesitantly or doubtfully. You are not a cringing suppliant but a child of God your Father, whom He welcomes into His presence at all times.

When you come on this basis, God offers you two things: mercy and grace. Neither of these can be earned. They must be received as free gifts of God.

Mercy for the Past

Mercy takes care of the *past*. It covers all the mistakes and failures that make you feel unqualified. Once you have confessed and repented of all the sins you have committed, they will no longer be held against you.

Your own memory may still be haunted by scenes from the past that you recall all too vividly—times when you acted, or reacted, in a way unworthy of a father. But once you have repented and confessed these sins, the marvelous message of the Gospel is that *God no longer remembers them*.

This is expressed vividly and beautifully in Micah 7:18–19:

> Who is a God like You, pardoning iniquity and passing over the transgression of the remnant of His heritage? He does not retain His anger forever, because He delights in mercy. He will again have compassion on us, and will subdue our iniquities. You will cast all our sins into the depths of the sea.

When you have met God's conditions, He casts your sins behind His back into the ocean of His forgetfulness. It was Corrie ten Boom who added, "And when God casts our sins into the ocean, He puts up a sign: *No fishing!*" If almighty God has forgotten your sins, why should you try to remember them?

Grace for the Future

Once your past has been dealt with, you can look to the *future* for the grace you need to succeed in your calling as a father. Grace, like mercy, can never be earned; it can be received only by faith.

Grace has been defined as "God's free, unmerited favor toward the undeserving and the ill-deserving." Because of your relationship to God through Jesus Christ, God looks on you with *favor*. He takes pleasure in you. He wants the best for you. He desires you to succeed in all circumstances—in particular as a father.

The apostle Paul endured tremendous trials and pressures. At one point he cried out to God for relief, but God's answer was, "My grace is sufficient for you" (2 Corinthians 12:9). It will be sufficient for you, too! Probably you will not have to experience all that Paul went through. But whatever your situation and experience, God's message to Paul is still true today: "My grace is sufficient for you."

Grace takes us beyond our own natural abilities. When we have exhausted our own resources, we can look to God for His grace—His supernatural enabling. Grace begins where our own ability ends.

This applies to you as a father. There will be times when you do not feel equal to your responsibilities. It is then that you will need to lay hold of God's grace. Acknowledge frankly to Him that you have exhausted your own resources, and tell Him, "Lord, I'm depending on You to be and to do what is otherwise impossible for me."

Then you will find, as Paul did, that when you have come to the end of your own resources, you have just begun to discover what God's grace can do. Then you, like the apostle, will be able to say, "When I am weak, then I am strong" (2 Corinthians 12:10).

3. Study Your Job Description

Perhaps you may need to read once more through chapters 8, 9 and 10, which deal with the responsibility of a father as the *priest, prophet* and *king* of his family. Make notes on the areas of your special weakness. Then pray and ask God to show you how you may do better.

But remember, God is on your side. He is pleased with your decision to accept your responsibility as head of your family. Remember, too, that when we depend totally on Him, we discover that He is totally dependable!

4. Give Your Job All the Time It Takes

One of the surest measures of our true priorities is the way we apportion our time. Certainly that is one of the ways our children determine how much they really mean to us. In contemporary Western society we find ourselves under ever-increasing pressures. We tend to measure our success by how quickly we perform given tasks. But that is not an accurate way to measure success in personal relationships—least of all in relationships with our children!

I read an account of a father and mother, both successful in their careers. One was a lawyer, the other in some kind of business. Their goal, like that of many parents today, was to give their two or three children a relatively small portion of their time, but to make sure the time they did give was "quality time." In other words, they would focus intensively on their children during the "quality time" allotted to them.

I did not get a clear impression of exactly what they would do with their children during this "quality time." But my personal reaction was that if I were a child, I would not be satisfied with a rationed amount of so-called quality time. What I would want—and what I believe every child wants—is to feel that my parents were *available* to me, that they were there when I needed them.

Some of us who are parents—and especially fathers—should ask ourselves how we would feel if God, our heavenly Father, gave us only a rationed portion of His time in which He was available to us. How grateful I am to know that our heavenly Father is not like that! He is always available, day or night. His promise is: "Before they call, I will answer; and while they are still speaking, I will hear" (Isaiah 65:24).

Obviously those of us who are fathers have many limitations. Some of these are purely physical; others are due to claims on our time that we cannot ignore. What is ultimately decisive is not the exact number of hours we are able to spend each day with our children, but that they feel we are *available* to them, and that when they speak, we really hear what they have to say. Can we assure them, as God assures us, "While they are still speaking, I will hear"?

Many years ago, while Lydia and I still had most of our children with us at home, we were sitting as a family around our dining table, sharing informally about the things of God. One of my daughters, about ten, was sitting on my knee. Quite unexpectedly—and without anyone praying for her—she received a sovereign, supernatural visitation of the Holy Spirit and began to worship the Lord in a new language that the Spirit Himself gave her.

Later I asked myself, *Why was it at that particular moment that she opened up to the Holy Spirit?* I concluded that it was because at that moment, while sitting on my knee, she felt totally accepted and secure. Every barrier to the Holy Spirit had been broken down.

As fathers we each need to ask ourselves: *Is the atmosphere in my home one of acceptance and security?* It will take more than brief periods of "quality time" to create that kind of atmosphere in your home. And it may require some sacrifice on your part. You may have to give up—temporarily, at least—some cherished hobby or sport. But when you do, you will be communicating with your child in a wordless language. You will be saying, "This is how important I think you are!"

15

Spiritual Fatherhood

I commented in chapter 8 that a real father is the most perfect depiction of God that any man can achieve, because fatherhood is the ultimate revelation of God Himself. Some might take offense at this. "But I'm not married," a man might say. Or, "I'm married but I have no children. Does that mean I can never become truly Godlike?"

Thank God the answer is no! You may never become a father in the natural, physical way. But another form of fatherhood remains open to you: *spiritual fatherhood*. By this I mean a form of fatherhood that comes out of a spiritual, nonphysical relationship. Nor is this by any means an inferior, second-class kind of fatherhood. In fact, some of the most significant characters in the Bible exemplified spiritual fatherhood.

The first and most outstanding example is Abraham. He was the father of natural children, of course, by Hagar, Sarah and finally Keturah. But beyond that, Scripture holds up Abraham before us as a pattern of spiritual fatherhood.

In Romans 4:13 Paul tells us, "The promise that he would be the heir of the world was not to Abraham or to his seed through the law, but through the righteousness of faith." He continues:

> Therefore it is of faith that it might be according to grace, so that the promise might be sure to all the seed, not only to those who are of the law, but also to those who are of the faith of Abraham, who is the father of us all (as it is written, "I have made you a father of many nations") in the presence of Him whom he believed, even God, who gives life to the dead and calls those things which do not exist as though they did; who, contrary to hope, in hope believed, so that he became the father of many nations, according to what was spoken, "So shall your descendants be."
>
> verses 16–18

In a spiritual sense, therefore, Abraham became the father of many nations. On what basis was this honor credited to him? On the basis of steadfast, unwavering faith expressed in wholehearted obedience. This found its ultimate expression in Abraham's response to God's requirement that he offer his son Isaac to Him as a sacrifice.

In this way Abraham marked out a path for all subsequent believers to follow. In Romans 4:20 Paul emphasized the steadfastness of Abraham's faith: "He did not waver at the promise of God through unbelief, but was strengthened in faith, giving glory to God."

The Pattern of Paul

Another outstanding example of spiritual fatherhood is provided by the apostle Paul. In 1 Corinthians 4:14–16 he wrote to the Christians in Corinth:

I do not write these things to shame you, but as my beloved children I warn you. For though you might have ten thousand instructors in Christ, yet you do not have many fathers; for in Christ Jesus I have begotten you through the gospel. Therefore I urge you, imitate me.

In Corinth Paul fathered a multitude of spiritual children through the seed of the Gospel, which he sowed in their hearts. Thus a servant of God who preaches God's Word faithfully can beget many spiritual children.

We need to bear in mind, however, the principle stated by God at the beginning of creation in Genesis 1:29:

And God said, "See, I have given you every herb that yields seed which is on the face of all the earth, and every tree whose fruit yields seed; to you it shall be for food."

It is the *fruit* of a tree that yields seed. A sermon preached from a life that has borne no fruit contains no seed that can produce life in others. That is one reason there is so much preaching that yields a temporary, emotional response but no permanent fruit.

In Philippians 2:20–22 Paul illustrated another form of spiritual fatherhood. He said of his young coworker Timothy:

I have no one like-minded, who will sincerely care for your state. For all seek their own, not the things which are of Christ Jesus. But you know his proven character, that as a son with his father he served with me in the gospel.

Part of the account of Paul's second missionary journey given in Acts 16:1–3 indicates that when Paul first met Timothy in the region of Derbe and Lystra, Timothy was already a believer well reported on by the leaders of the local church. Discerning the spiritual potential in this young man, Paul invited him to join him in his further travels.

From that time on Timothy became Paul's most trusted coworker in a relationship that continued until Paul's death.

In this case Paul became a spiritual father to Timothy not by winning him to Christ through the Gospel, but by a personal relationship in which Paul took Timothy as a trusted coworker. In this way Timothy not only received spiritual instruction from Paul, but he followed him through the many different phases of Paul's ongoing ministry. He was an eyewitness of how Paul actually worked out his teaching in daily living under many different forms of pressure.

Near the end of his life Paul wrote to Timothy:

> You have carefully followed my doctrine, manner of life, purpose, faith, longsuffering, love, perseverance, persecutions, afflictions, which happened to me at Antioch, at Iconium, at Lystra—what persecutions I endured. And out of them all the Lord delivered me. Yes, and all who desire to live godly in Christ Jesus will suffer persecution.
>
> 2 Timothy 3:10–12

The instruction Timothy had received from Paul was not in the form of classroom lectures, but in all the ups and downs of a pressure-filled life. Timothy had not merely listened to Paul preaching. Much more important, he had seen firsthand how Paul actually practiced what he preached. It was out of this close personal association that Paul became a spiritual father to Timothy.

There were a number of other young men with whom Paul enjoyed a relationship like the one he had with Timothy, though perhaps not so close. These included Titus, Sopater from Berea, Aristarchus and Secundus from Thessalonica, Gaius from Derbe, Tychicus and Trophimus from Asia.

One of the things most needed in the contemporary Church is men who will fill the role Paul played in the life of Timothy. I have already pointed out the desperate need in our society for men who are truly fathers. The need is no less great in the Church. We have men who can organize, sermonize, administrate and perform all sorts of religious functions. But how many will give themselves to younger men and share with them both successes and sorrows in the rough and tumble of daily Christian living? How many are willing, if need be, to share their moments of weakness and disappointment?

In 1 Thessalonians Paul introduced what we might call a "third generation" of spiritual fatherhood. Paul spoke on behalf of Silas and Timothy as well as himself:

> You know how we exhorted, and comforted, and charged every one of you, as a father does his own children, that you would have a walk worthy of God who calls you into His own kingdom and glory.
>
> 1 Thessalonians 2:11–12

Timothy was associated here with Paul and Silas in filling the role of spiritual father in relationship to the Christians in Thessalonica. So a spiritual son of Paul now also figured as a spiritual father to the Thessalonians. This gives a total of three spiritual generations: Paul as a father to Timothy, who was in turn a father to the Thessalonians. This may be represented as follows:

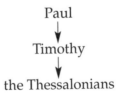

A Life of Faith and Obedience

In chapter 7 I pointed out that Jesus did not reveal the Father to His disciples as a theological concept. As He said in John 17:6, He "manifested" the name of the Father to them by the way He lived out His life before them. It was a life of unbroken communion with the Father, of moment-by-moment dependence on the Father and of unfailing obedience to the Father's will.

Likewise spiritual fatherhood cannot be merely a label or a theological concept. It is expressed by a life lived out in faith and obedience that becomes a pattern for others to follow.

A spiritual father must be able to give the same command Jesus gave His disciples: "Follow Me!" Or, as Paul told the Christians at Corinth, "Imitate me, just as I also imitate Christ" (1 Corinthians 11:1).

In the modern Israeli army the following rule has been established. A commander does not say to his troops, "Advance!" He says, "After me!" The same applies to the army of the Lord.

It is in the area of character that God subjects His servants to the most rigorous tests. We need to ask, therefore, what the character requirements are in a man who desires to fulfill the role of spiritual father. For an answer we may summarize briefly the main character features of the men we have held up as spiritual fathers.

Abraham

The aspects of Abraham's character that stand out, as I have noted, are his unwavering faith and his prompt, total obedience to all that God required of him. This is illustrated beautifully when God asked him for the sacrifice of his son, Isaac.

Undoubtedly Isaac was the dearest thing in Abraham's life. Also, as the writer of Hebrews points out, Isaac was to be the channel through whom Abraham was to receive all the blessings God had promised him. Nevertheless

Abraham did not waver. He not only obeyed; he obeyed *promptly*, without hesitation:

> Abraham rose *early in the morning* and saddled his donkey, and took two of his young men with him, and Isaac his son; and he split the wood for the burnt offering, and arose and went to the place of which God had told him.
>
> Genesis 22:3, emphasis added

Paul

Through the message of the Gospel, Paul became a father to many of the Christians in Corinth, for two reasons.

First, in his preaching, Paul did not offer, as some preachers do today, an easy and simplistic answer to life's problems. His message to the Corinthians focused on *the cross*. In 1 Corinthians 2:1–2 Paul emphasized this:

> And I, brethren, when I came to you, did not come with excellence of speech or of wisdom declaring to you the testimony of God. For I determined not to know anything among you except Jesus Christ and Him crucified.

Nor did Paul focus on the cross only in his preaching. More important, he had experienced the cross in his own life, as he wrote in Galatians 6:14:

> God forbid that I should glory except in the cross of our Lord Jesus Christ, by whom the world has been crucified to me, and I to the world.

Spiritual children were born to Paul in Corinth, then, because his message focused on the cross and because the cross was attested by his own life, in which he had subjected personal ambition and self-seeking to a ruthless process of self-crucifixion.

A crossless message from an uncrucified preacher, by contrast, will not produce the kind of spiritual children God granted to Paul in Corinth.

Paul, Silas and Timothy

We already saw that Paul, Silas and Timothy are portrayed in 1 Thessalonians as spiritual fathers. Paul wrote that the Thessalonians

> are witnesses, and God also, how devoutly and justly and blamelessly we behaved ourselves among you who believe; as you know how we exhorted, and comforted, and charged every one of you, as a father does his own children, that you would have a walk worthy of God who calls you into His own kingdom and glory.
>
> 1 Thessalonians 2:10–12

Paul emphasized two main aspects of the conduct of all three men. First, their example. Their personal lives were "blameless." Second, they had a father's heart toward the Thessalonians. Setting before them the highest standard, they continually challenged and exhorted their disciples to attain to that standard. Just as a natural father takes pride in the successes of his children, so these three men were eager to see their disciples develop into successful and fruitful Christians.

What Characteristics?

If we were to sum up the main features of the characters of the men listed above, we would arrive at a list something like this:

Unwavering faith
Prompt and total obedience

A message that focused on the cross
The cross applied in their own lives
Faultless Christian conduct
Fatherly affection for young believers
Zealous concern for their true success

Practical Fatherhood: Adoption

Another kind of fatherhood falls somewhere between natural, physical fatherhood, on the one hand, and the purely spiritual kind of fatherhood I have been describing, on the other. I speak of the actual adoption, either legal or *de facto*, of children whose parents either cannot or will not care for them.

In this connection I am continuously reminded of the definition James gives of the kind of religion that is acceptable to God:

> Pure and undefiled religion before God and the Father is this: to visit orphans and widows in their trouble, and to keep oneself unspotted from the world.
>
> James 1:27

Observe the distinction between religion and salvation. Salvation is what God does for man. Religion is what man does in return for God. Our religion is our response to God's salvation.

Recently my mind has returned continually to this verse in the epistle of James. I find it truly amazing that millions of Bible-believing Christians seem never to have heard what James is saying in this verse. In describing the kind of religious activity that pleases God, he begins with the positive—that is, the things God expects us to do. The first thing James speaks of is visiting—caring and providing for—orphans and widows. At the end he moves on to the negative, concluding by exhorting his readers "to keep [themselves] unspotted from the world."

I have been listening to sermons from a great variety of preachers for more than fifty years. I have heard many messages, often preached with great fervor, on the need to keep oneself unspotted from the world. I do not recall that I have ever heard a sermon preached on our obligation to care for orphans and widows.

Yet our responsibility to care for orphans and widows is emphasized continually throughout the whole Bible, both under the Old Covenant and under the New. As I have analyzed the message of the Old Testament prophets, I have concluded that there are three main sins that offend God. The first is idolatry; the second, adultery; the third, failure to care for orphans and widows. It seems to me that God puts them all on the same level.

It is true that the first two are sins of *commission* and the third is a sin of *omission*. But that does not make the third any less serious. We are just as guilty for the good things we do not do as for the bad things we do.

Certainly it is not through lack of opportunity that we fail to care for orphans and widows. They are multiplying all over the world. As this book is published there are several million AIDS orphans in Uganda alone. And that is only one relatively small country on the vast continent of Africa. When the AIDS plague makes its full impact on the subcontinent of India, its toll will be even more horrific than in Africa.

Some Western Christians might adopt the attitude, "That's a problem of backward, uncivilized nations. We're not responsible for them."

I disagree. I believe that I am my brother's keeper, whatever the color of his skin or the country he lives in. Even so, however, the problem of orphans and widows is not confined to nations in the developing world. The problem is just as serious, in a different form, in the nations of the West. In chapter 12 I pointed out that we are confronted by ever increasing millions of unparented young people—children who have "gone into captivity" because their fathers failed in their responsibilities. By the dictionary definition these children may not technically be orphans, but their needs are just as great.

The progressive breakup of the family in the West is producing more and more single parents. In most cases these are mothers, not fathers. People sometimes suggest that their difficulties are the result of their own sinful conduct. It is true, some of their children have been conceived out of wedlock. But where in the Gospels did Jesus ever forbid us to show mercy to sinners? Furthermore the ones suffering the most are the unparented children—who are not the ones who sinned. In addition, multitudes of women are single mothers through no fault of their own. They were legally married, bore their husbands one or more children, then were abandoned without valid reason.

Yet the contemporary Church is paying little attention, for the most part, to the vast number of single parents. I can believe that the Lord would say to us just what He said to Israel in Isaiah's day:

> "Wash yourselves, make yourselves clean; put away the evil of your doings from before My eyes. Cease to do evil, learn to do good; seek justice, reprove the oppressor; defend the fatherless, plead for the widow."
>
> Isaiah 1:16–17

Some contemporary Christians would not agree that the opening words apply to them. But, as I have said, we are just as guilty for the good we do not do as for the evil we do. We must also bear in mind that the people Isaiah was addressing were extremely religious. God had just finished saying to them:

> "Bring no more futile sacrifices; incense is an abomination to Me. The New Moons, the Sabbaths, and the calling of

assemblies—I cannot endure iniquity and the sacred meeting. Your New Moons and your appointed feasts My soul hates; they are a trouble to Me, I am weary of bearing them."

verse 13

In Luke 6:46 Jesus brought a similar charge against the religious people of His day. He did not reprove them for what they were doing, but for what they were not doing: "Why do you call Me 'Lord, Lord' and do not do the things which I say?"

Many in our Western society have become cynical about Christianity, considering it an irrelevant carryover from previous generations. They feel it has nothing to offer the problems we face today. These people are not impressed by sermons. They demand to see the Gospel produce positive, practical results.

One visible, objective contribution the Church could make is a practical demonstration of fatherhood, in the various forms I have depicted. Multitudes of young people in our society today realize there is something missing in their lives. They are searching for it in various places: in alcohol, in drugs, in gangs and cliques, in the occult, in bizarre religions and philosophies and in violent computer games.

What they are actually looking for, although they do not know it, is a father.

16

Where Are the Spiritual Fathers?

In the last two decades of the twentieth century, two world-famous evangelists carried out careful analyses of the people who had responded to their preaching in their mass crusades and who had been registered as converts. Many assistants and large sums of money were involved in the presentation and organization of their evangelistic campaigns and the subsequent follow-up of their converts. It could be said that no effort or expense was spared. Yet the results of their analyses were sobering. One evangelist concluded that five percent of his converts actually became committed Christians; the other evangelist, only three percent.

Let me emphasize that these figures were not arrived at by some secular agency that might have been prejudiced against evangelism. In each case the surveys were carried out by the evangelist's own organization. I need to emphasize, too, that I am not criticizing either of these evangelists. They are men of proven integrity whom I esteem highly as brothers in the Lord.

We do need to ask, however, what would happen in the secular world if any business received five percent or less of their anticipated return from some project in which they had made a major investment. Almost certainly such a business would end up in bankruptcy. Would it be fair to conclude that the contemporary Church, as represented by these statistics, is spiritually bankrupt?

The lack of enduring results cannot be attributed to any defect in the evangelistic message preached, since each emphasized the necessity of the new birth and included a clear-cut presentation of salvation. There was perhaps one point in which the message fell short of the New Testament pattern: There was relatively little emphasis on the judgment of God on sin. But this by itself would not account for the lack of permanent fruit.

The main reason for such disappointing results, I believe, lies in the condition of the contemporary Church as a whole. At one time, while serving as a pastor, I was enrolled as a counselor for new converts from a major evangelistic campaign in my area that was claiming impressive results. Our responsibility as counselors was not only to talk with the inquirers in the meetings, but to maintain ongoing contact with every person we counseled—by phone calls, by letters, by offers of hospitality.

For my part I counseled 22 persons, of whom I kept a careful record. At the end, after using every means of follow-up available to me, I concluded that only two persons had actually become committed Christians. Both of these became members of my congregation. I followed their lives for many years after. Both developed into stable, fruitful Christians.

What was the reason for the success of these two? Certainly not that I was pastoring a large, impressive congregation. The number of our members at that time did not exceed fifty! Eventually I concluded that the decisive factor was that, however imperfectly, I offered both of them some kind of spiritual fatherhood.

Concerning the other twenty persons I counseled, I determined that their failure to mature into committed Christians was due to one or the other of two causes: either they never became attached to any congregation, or else they became attached to a congregation that did not offer them spiritual fatherhood. Concerning this situation at that time, a religious commentator remarked, "It doesn't make sense to put a live chick under a dead hen!"

Christianity or Churchianity?

Nearly twenty centuries have elapsed since Jesus commissioned and sent out His first apostles. During that time a tremendous change has taken place in the Christian world, which for the most part has gone unnoticed. We have substituted *churchianity* for *Christianity*. Churchianity produces *church members;* Christianity produces *disciples*. Churchianity demands *conformity;* Christianity demands *commitment*. The great majority of professing Christians today are not even aware of their departure from the original pattern and standard of the Gospel. They have simply formed their concept of Christianity from what they see in the contemporary Church.

When Jesus sent out those first apostles, His instructions were perfectly clear:

> "Go . . . and make *disciples* of all the nations."
>
> Matthew 28:19, emphasis added

Previously He had given an unequivocal definition of what becoming His disciple involved:

Where Are the Spiritual Fathers?

> Large crowds were going along with Him; and He
> turned and said to them, "If anyone comes to Me, and does
> not hate his own father and mother and wife and children
> and brothers and sisters, yes, and even his own life, he can-
> not be My disciple. Whoever does not carry his own cross
> and come after Me cannot be My disciple.
>
> Luke 14:25–27, NASB

This passage makes a pointed contrast between two
kinds of people: the great multitudes, on the one hand,
who were "going along with Him"; and the single individual, on the other hand, who "[comes] after Me."
Churchianity is satisfied with great multitudes who go
along with Jesus. Christianity focuses primarily on each
individual who comes after Jesus. It is concerned to produce not fellow travelers but committed followers.

From my experience in counseling, which I described
above, and from other similar circumstances, I eventually
came to see that it takes spiritual fathering to form new
converts into committed Christians. It is the rare convert
who rises to a spiritual level higher than that of the church
he or she attends. Where there is no effective spiritual
fathering, the majority of new converts will remain spiritual orphans, never becoming mature, fruitful members of
God's family.

In chapter 12, "When Fathers Fail," I described the conditions that prevail among young people who have never
been properly fathered: lack of discipline, lack of clear focus,
vulnerability to every kind of satanic lure and deception.
Conditions in the contemporary Church, in many respects,
closely parallel those in the world. Many young people who
say they are saved demonstrate the same lack of focus as
their counterparts in the world. They are carried to and fro
by every changing fashion in speech, clothing, entertainment, even styles of worship. For these young people, worship is a form of religious self-expression. Seldom do they

see it as a personal encounter with a holy and awesome God. For the most part their lives lack two things: stability and any clearly defined goal.

In our contemporary culture three characteristics are common to youth, whether in the world or in the Church.

Disillusionment

First, they are *disillusioned*—about the state of society, about the condition of the planet, about the lack of social justice and provision for the weaker members of society. The preceding generations have failed them, they feel, and bequeathed them problems for which they see no solutions.

I have to acknowledge, speaking as a member of a previous generation, that in this respect, at least, the young people are right. We have passed on to them a culture and society that are in many ways the outcome of our own sins—greed, selfishness, indifference to the weak and helpless. Although many of us call ourselves Christians, we have failed to fulfill the first duty of "pure and undefiled religion": to care for the orphans and widows. If we urge on the rising generation the claims of the Christian faith, they could well respond, "First practice what you preach; then we'll listen to what you have to say."

Looking for Pure Gold

A second mark of today's young people is that they are *looking for what is genuine*. If we offer them gold, they will take a knife and scratch deep below the surface to see whether it is gold all the way through, or simply gold overlaying a base metal.

Of the seven churches portrayed in Revelation 2 and 3, probably the one closest to the contemporary Western church is the church of Laodicea. It was to this church, you recall, that Jesus said, "I counsel you to buy from Me gold refined in the fire" (Revelation 3:18). There is much gold in the contemporary Church that has never passed through the test of the fire. We preach eloquent sermons and make high-sounding claims, but all too often, when the fire is applied, the gold does not pass the test.

A Radical Response

A third mark of today's young people is that they are *radical*. They are not looking for easy, superficial answers. They are unimpressed by the established order or by long-standing traditions. In a sense nothing is sacred to them. If a tree is producing rotten fruit, or no fruit, their response is simple: "Cut it down!" (They would have responded to the preaching of John the Baptist!) Their condition is a desperate, unspoken cry for the reality of spiritual fatherhood.

Out of Weakness Made Strong

At this point I can hear someone respond, "But the standards you've described for spiritual fathers are so high! I could never be an Abraham or a Paul."

It is true, God's standards are high. Nor does He ever lower them. But something else is also true: God's grace is always sufficient. For every task God assigns, He gives the grace needed to carry it out.

Abraham and Paul are set forth in Scripture not as standards to attain to but as examples to follow. In Romans 4:12 Paul said that Abraham is our father if we "walk in the steps of [his] faith." Abraham has marked out a path of faith, in other words, on which all believers are called to follow.

We have already noted Paul's exhortation to "imitate me, just as I also imitate Christ" (1 Corinthians 11:1). If

God's grace could so transform Saul, the arch persecutor of Christians, that he became an imitator of Christ, then God's grace can so change you that you can become an imitator of Paul. The apostle stated in 1 Timothy 1:16 that this was the very purpose for which he was saved: "That in me first Jesus Christ might show all longsuffering, as a pattern to those who are going to believe on Him for everlasting life."

Expressed in simple language, Paul was saying, "If God could change me, He can change anyone!"

Remember, too, that both Abraham and Paul had their moments of weakness. Abraham made some serious mistakes. At one point he so despaired of having a son and heir by his wife, Sarah, that he conceived a son by Sarah's maid. Later, to protect his own life, he told Abimelech, king of Gerar, that Sarah was his sister, and allowed her to be taken into Abimelech's harem. Only God's supernatural intervention saved Sarah from becoming one of Abimelech's wives (see Genesis 20).

Yet God never gave up on Abraham. And so, by God's grace, he eventually became what God had declared he would be.

Paul, too, had his moments of great weakness. In 2 Corinthians 1:8–9 Paul said, concerning himself and his companions:

> We were burdened beyond measure, above strength, so that we despaired even of life. Yes, we had the sentence of death in ourselves, that we should not trust in ourselves but in God who raises the dead.

God permitted Paul to come to a place of such total weakness that he would no longer trust in himself, but in Him who can even raise the dead.

Later in the same epistle, Paul related how he learned that God's strength is made perfect in our weakness. Finally he came to the conclusion,

Where Are the Spiritual Fathers?

When I am weak, then I am strong.

2 Corinthians 12:10

Both Abraham and Paul—it is true—are set forth as examples of spiritual fathers. But they became spiritual fathers only when they came to the end of their own abilities and relied on God's supernatural grace. That is still true today. Men can become spiritual fathers only when they respond to a desire that God Himself has put into their hearts, and when they come to the end of their own resources and rely on His supernatural enabling.

In Matthew 4:19 Jesus said to Peter and Andrew, "Follow Me, and I will make you fishers of men." The same principle holds true today. What is important in our lives is not what we are in ourselves, but what Jesus can make us if we follow Him.

Do you see young people around you whose unstable, directionless lives are a wordless cry for help? Have you come to realize that what they need is a spiritual father? Do you long to help them? Then you need to understand that it is God Himself who has put this desire into your heart. He wants to make you a spiritual father.

Once you realize this is God's plan for you, then what you are in yourself is no longer important. What is important is what God can make you, once you yield yourself fully to Him. In your own way and in your own words, simply tell God that you are available to Him. He will do the rest!

145

17

A Word to the Fatherless

As you have read through the preceding chapters, possibly you have realized that you have never known a father such as I have been depicting. If so, let me assure you that in the world today are millions more like you.

Each of us has a biological father, of course, a source from which our physical life proceeded. But that by no means guarantees that we have had a father such as is portrayed in Scripture and as I have been seeking to describe in this book. In fact, fathers answering to that description in today's world are rare!

If you have not had such a father, then somewhere deep down inside you there is a void—an emptiness that has never been filled. It may be so deep down, and it may have been there so long, that you are not consciously aware of it. Nevertheless it is there, and because of it you are an incomplete person.

I am not suggesting that you need necessarily have had a perfect father. Actually there is only one perfect father— God the Father in heaven. But an earthly father who answers to the biblical description, even though he may be in many ways imperfect, nevertheless fills up that void inside you. As a result you are not fatherless; you know in personal experience what it is to have a father.

But, as I said, millions do not.

Will it help you if I share from personal experience? My father, like every other male relative I have known, was an officer in the British Army. He was a moral, honest man, faithful in his duties, a successful soldier. Because he served with the British Army in India, it was there that I was born, in the city of Bangalore.

When I was born, the doctor told my mother that she should not expect to have any more children. This meant I would grow up without brothers or sisters. My parents decided, therefore, that the best way to supply this lack was for my father to relate to me as an older brother, rather than as a parent. Apparently they considered it more important for me to have a brother than a father. The result was that I never addressed him as Father or Daddy, but only by his first name, Peter. I do not doubt that he loved me, but he never showed any warm affection for me. I do not recall that he ever took me on his knees or cuddled me.

In World War II, at age 25, I had a personal encounter with Jesus Christ in a barrack room of the British Army. As a result I became a committed Christian. This experience opened me up to the reality of spiritual forces of which, up to that time, I had been completely unaware.

In particular I realized that India, the land of my birth, is the vortex of a swirling mass of immensely powerful spiritual forces, all of which are non-Christian. I had the impression that some of those spiritual forces from India had been following me up through my life, seeking to gain control over me. They never succeeded, yet I was never completely free from their influence. Before becoming a committed Christian, I had actually for a time contemplated becoming a yogi.

Studying the Bible as a Christian, I learned that through the new birth God had become my Father. In fact, later I preached a series of three messages on tape on the theme "Knowing God as Father." Various people have told me that these messages have helped them. And yet, though I did not know it, I was preaching only a theory. I understood this doctrine clearly, yet still had no experiential knowledge of God as really being my Father. I was not even aware of what was lacking in my life.

A Personal Revelation

Then, in 1996, just after I had celebrated fifty years in full-time Christian ministry, God intervened in my life. One morning Ruth and I were sitting up in bed, praying together as we normally did, when I was sovereignly touched by supernatural power. I found myself the battleground of two opposing spiritual forces.

Stretched out over me from behind was an invisible arm, holding something like a black skullcap that it was seeking to press down over my head. At the same time the power of the Holy Spirit began to move through my body. Starting at my feet, it moved upward through me. My body began to shake violently. Ruth told me later that the skin of my face turned deep red. I had the impression that these two spiritual forces were in opposition to each other. The power of the Holy Spirit moving upward through me was working against the arm above me that was attempting to press the skullcap down on my head.

Eventually the Holy Spirit prevailed. The arm with the skullcap was forced back and disappeared. At the same time the Holy Spirit took full control of my body, and I had a marvelous sense of relaxation and of peace.

Simultaneously, without any conscious process of reasoning, I discovered that for the first time in my life I was aware of a direct, intimate relationship with God as my Father. Immediately it was absolutely natural to address Him as Father. This was no longer a theological statement but the spontaneous expression of a personal relationship.

As I was meditating on this experience, I concluded that the arm with the skullcap was a manifestation of Shiva, one of the three main Hindu "gods" (which are, of course, no gods at all, but evil satanic powers in the heavenlies).

My understanding of what had happened to me was remarkably confirmed about two years later, when I happened to be reading a description of the main "gods" of Hinduism. It depicted Shiva as a spiritual force that comes down over a person's head and shuts him off from the realities of the heavenly realm. This was exactly what that arm stretched out over my head had been seeking to do to me. How grateful I am that in the moment of crisis, the Holy Spirit came to my help and dispelled the evil power seeking to take control of me!

Ever since that experience in 1996, my relationship with God as my Father has steadily become stronger and more intimate.

A New Relationship

My new relationship has had a profound, ongoing effect on my life. I had been serving Christ to the best of my ability for more than fifty years, during which time God had granted much fruit from my ministry. But through entering this new relationship with God as my Father, I began to experience an intimacy in my relationship with Him, and a degree of security, that I had never known before.

This new relationship did not exempt me from the tests that come into every Christian life, but it did enable me to meet those tests with a greater measure of inward strength and confidence. Furthermore my tests did not come between me and God; they merely drew me closer to Him.

About three years after the experience I have described, I endured one of the most painful experiences of my entire Christian life. After more than a month in an intensive care unit, God took my precious wife, Ruth, home to Himself. My sense of loss was indescribable. Yet in the midst of it all, I never for a moment lost the awareness of my Father's loving presence with me.

At the interment service, as I looked down onto the casket containing Ruth's body in the grave, I felt impelled to cry out in the presence of all the mourners, "Father, I trust You. I thank You that You are always kind and loving and just. You never make a mistake. What You do is always the best."

Only my intimate awareness of God as my Father enabled me to make that confession. Several people who had been present told me later how powerfully it had affected them.

I do not want to give you the impression, however, that in order to know God in a personal way as your Father, you will have to pass through the same kind of experience. God deals with us all as individuals. There is no standard procedure that all must follow. There are, however, certain scriptural principles that do apply in every life.

In Matthew 11:27 Jesus lays down the principles that apply first to knowing Him as the Son of God and then to knowing God as His Father:

> "All things have been delivered to Me by My Father, and no one knows the Son except the Father. Nor does anyone know the Father except the Son, and he to whom the Son wills to reveal Him."

The Father and Son act in mutual cooperation with one another. First the Father reveals the Son. This is the first step, for it is only through the Son that we can come to know the Father. In John 14:6 Jesus says, "No one comes to the Father except through Me." After that comes the second step, when Jesus reveals the Father—but only at the discretion of His sovereign will. Jesus emphasizes that the revelation of the Father is given only to those whom "the Son *wills* to reveal Him" (Matthew 11:27, emphasis added).

Jesus is speaking here about a *revelation* that only He can give. It is important to note the difference between knowing Scripture as a *doctrine* and knowing it by *revelation*. For more than fifty years I honestly accepted the *doctrine* that God was my Father. But it was altogether different when I received this as a direct personal *revelation*.

Through the Son to the Father

Perhaps after reading this far, you have come to realize that you are *fatherless*. You have never known what it is to have a real father. Now there is a stirring in your heart— a longing for a father.

It may be that through the circumstances of your past, no human being in your life will ever be a real father to you. All the more reason to thank God that there is a heavenly Father whom you can come to know! But first you must know Jesus as your personal Savior, through whom you have received the gift of eternal life.

1. Receive Jesus as Savior

If you do not already have this scriptural assurance, the first step is to receive Jesus as your personal Savior. This is clearly stated in John 1:11–13:

He [Jesus] came to His own, and His own did not receive Him. But as many as received Him, to them He gave the right to become children of God, even to those who believe in His name: who were born, not of blood, nor of the will of the flesh, nor of the will of man, but of God.

At this point, if you wish, you may pray a simple prayer something like this:

Lord Jesus Christ, I acknowledge You as the Son of God and the only way to God. I believe that You died on the cross to pay the penalty for my sins, and that You rose again from the dead. I ask you now to forgive all my sins, and I receive you by faith as my personal Savior. Come into my heart and give me the gift of eternal life. Amen.

When you pray that prayer in simple faith, God promises to give you an inward assurance that He has received you as His child. In 1 John 5:10 the apostle tells us that "he who believes in the Son of God has the witness in himself." Again, in Romans 8:16, Paul tells us, "The Spirit Himself [that is, God's Holy Spirit] bears witness with our spirit that we are children of God."

Begin now in faith to thank God that He has received you and that you are His child. The more you thank Him, the more real it will become to you that you have truly become a child of God. The Holy Spirit will bear witness with your spirit that this is so.

2. Approach God as Father

Now Jesus has become for you the door through whom you may boldly approach God. You are open to receive the personal revelation of God as your heavenly Father, which Jesus alone can give you.

I shared that I lived as a born-again Christian for more than fifty years before entering into the personal revelation of God as my Father. I am not for one moment suggesting, however, that any other Christian needs to wait that long! One main purpose of my writing this book, in fact, is to help Christians enter much sooner into this revelation.

Nevertheless each of us is totally dependent on Jesus to grant us this revelation. He Himself said so emphatically: "Nor does anyone know the Father except the Son, and he to whom the Son wills to reveal Him" (Matthew 11:27). It is extremely healthy for each of us to come to the place where we acknowledge our total dependence on God.

Some contemporary versions of the Gospel depict God as a heavenly automatic vending machine. When you put in the coins and press the right buttons, out comes what you are seeking from Him. But God is not an automatic vending machine. He is a Father who disciplines His children and sets certain standards of behavior. One of the disciplines He requires is that we humble ourselves before Him: "God resists the proud, but gives grace to the humble" (1 Peter 5:5).

Another discipline we must learn is to wait on God. The time that suits us is not always God's appointed time. "Those who wait on the LORD shall renew their strength" (Isaiah 40:31). More than once I have set out to count all the promises Scripture offers those willing to wait on God, but I have never succeeded. There are too many!

In my case I can believe that God withheld the revelation from me until He knew I was ready to receive it. Certainly when He did grant it to me, I received it as a treasure worth waiting for!

Ask, Seek, Knock

It may be that you have already received this intimate, personal knowledge of God as your Father, which only Jesus can give. I have no way of knowing. Then again, you may be in the same condition I was in. You know beyond a shadow of a doubt that you are born again. To the best of your understanding and ability, you are serving the Lord sincerely. Yet you have a hunger for something beyond your present experience—for a deep, intimate, abiding relationship with God as your Father.

I want to encourage you to press through to all God has stored up for you. Take time in the presence of Jesus. Open up to Him the deepest longings of your heart. Ask Him to show you if there are unsuspected hindrances coming between you and Him. Be prepared for Him to lead you in paths along which you have never walked. Yield yourself unreservedly to Him.

At the same time do not entertain any preconceived ideas of how God will meet you. In my case the revelation of God's Fatherhood came with a powerful supernatural experience. But God may deal with you altogether differently. You may be like Elijah on Mount Horeb, waiting to hear from God (see 1 Kings 19:11–18).

First there were three demonstrations of supernatural power: a wind, an earthquake and a fire. But God was in none of them. These were followed by a "still small voice" (verse 12). The NIV translates it "a gentle whisper." It was in this quiet, undramatic way that God came to Elijah. Yet when Elijah heard Him, he covered his face with his mantle in reverential awe.

There is more power in God's whisper than in the mightiest wind or earthquake or fire! That may be how God will deal with you.

Regardless, let me encourage you with a word of counsel from Jesus. In each case the form of the verb He uses indicates that He is speaking of repeated or continuous action:

> "Ask [and keep on asking], and it will be given to you; seek [and keep on seeking], and you will find; knock [and keep on knocking], and it will be opened to you."
>
> Matthew 7:7

Remember, it *will* be given to you; you *will* find; it *will* be opened to you.

In the next verse Jesus follows up with a further word of assurance and encouragement:

> "For everyone who asks receives, and he who seeks finds, and to him who knocks it will be opened."

That word *everyone* includes you!

*   *   *   *   *

Before you close this book, briefly review its main theme.

The most complete revelation of God through human beings is through the institution of the family. The love between husband and wife mirrors the relationship between Jesus and His Church. The love of a father for his family mirrors the love God has for all He has created. It is in the outworking of God's plan for the family that His highest good is made available to man. But through the rejection of God's plan for the family, human misery reaches its zenith.

This is an issue to which our contemporary culture must determine how it will respond. It is also an issue to which you as an individual must respond.

Subject Index

Scripture Index